OUR LORD
and
OUR LADY
IN SCOTTSDALE

Fruitful Charisms in a
Traditional American Parish

by
Fr. René Laurentin

Translated from original French manuscript by
Doris Laguette, B.A., French Literature,
University of California, Irvine
Ernesto V. Laguette, B.S., Electrical Engineering,
University of New Hampshire

Edited and Published by
FAITH PUBLISHING COMPANY
P.O. Box 237
Milford, Ohio 45150

The Publisher recognizes and accepts that the final authority regarding the apparitions at St. Maria Goretti Parish rests with the Holy See of Rome, to whose judgment we willingly submit.

—The Publisher

Published by Faith Publishing Company
For additional copies, write to:
Faith Publishing Company
P.O. Box 237
Milford, Ohio 45150, or to,

The Riehle Foundation
P.O. Box 7
Milford, Ohio 45150

Copyright © 1992 Faith Publishing Company

Library of Congress Catalog Card No.: 92-071737

ISBN: 1-880033-02-X

TABLE OF CONTENTS

iii

Acknowledgements

TO his Excellency Thomas Joseph O'Brien, in union with his pastoral welcome and his prudence.

TO Bill Reck, concerned about informing and distributing the fruits of Scottsdale and who led me to write this book and who has contributed to its documentation.

TO Doris and Ernesto Laguette who helped at all stages of this research and have done the translation.

TO Carol Ameche to whom we owe the first archives of the events.

TO the visionaries and to the persons I have met in the course of my two trips to Scottsdale.

TO the opponents with whom I dialogued constantly, and those who had been accused of opposing but denied it.

TO Father Robert Faricy whom Bill Reck had put me in touch with, and with whom my relationship was but a friendly confidence and a shared concern to serve discernment.

TO Father Jack Spaulding who after having awakened the deaf-mutes to the language of faith, awakened the parish to the charisms which the Church of today needs, keeping prudence and obedience.

THE AUTHOR WISHES TO EXPRESS HIS HEARTFELT GRATITUDE.

Publisher's Foreword

For over four decades, Fr. René Laurentin has devoted endless hours to the study of apparitions and to the role of the Blessed Virgin Mary in the salvation of mankind. His work has taken him around the world many times.

In 1990 and 1991, recognizing the incredible demand for the three Volumes of the book titled, *I Am Your Jesus of Mercy*, Fr. Laurentin began his inquiry of the events occurring at St. Maria Goretti Parish in Scottsdale, Arizona.

The proliferation of claimed apparitions and messages from the heavens in the past twenty years is staggering, and it seems to have reached a crescendo during the 1980s and on into this decade. We are constantly bombarded with new reports, or manuscripts depicting new messages to the world from Our Lord or Our Lady. Even if we should rule out the authenticity of most of them, the remaining are enough to cause us to take a long, hard look at who is trying to get our attention, and why.

The world teeters precariously in the face of a dozen different dilemmas and is steeped in sin, violence and poverty. The family unit is disintegrating, the Church becomes more divided in controversy. Our natural reaction is to plead for assistance from Him who created us and our world. But how often we question His method of response. How often we rule out the possibility of His presence through the apparitions and messages He is providing.

In contrast, the people of faith seem to respond with hope and zeal. The great increase in devotion to Our Lady, the return to the use of the Rosary, and the proliferation of prayer groups springing up all over the world, give evidence to it. Such is the success of the *I Am Your Jesus of Mercy* books. The responses we receive regarding the books are an absolute confirmation that people are searching for spiritual food—a hunger that is not being fed from the pulpit today.

In reporting his findings at Scottsdale, Fr. Laurentin delves into this current situation. In this book, he provides far more than just information or the results of investigation of the events, but instead, he gives it all meaning, purpose, detailing the need and reason for our spiritual hunger. In these pages we will see how the events at Scottsdale might be an answer to that hunger, giving us a detailed blueprint of what we need to do, and how we are to do it.

As is the case with all of his writings, Fr. Laurentin is not satisfied with simply reporting the facts of the events. He strives to tell us "why." In the following pages, he goes into great depth to tell us why.

Bill Reck
Faith Publishing Co.

INTRODUCTION

Why This Book?

Why write a book about the spiritual events that are happening in Scottsdale, a suburb of Phoenix, in the desert of Arizona?

It is because this presence of Jesus and Mary in a strong and traditional American Parish brings to the Church in the United States a model of renewal, not by a pastoral ideology or criticism, but by prayer and by listening to the living voice and messages of Jesus and Mary.

While traveling in the United States, especially during my last trip there, what I found astonishing was a steady increase of prayer and spiritual fervor, generously sustained in many localities. Let us situate this phenomenon in the Catholic Church's recent history, for it is an indication of God's plans. Thus, I provide a brief synopsis of the American Church for the past 25 years.

The American Church Before Vatican II

Before the Second Vatican Council, the American Church was solid, generous (finacially and otherwise) but reasonably formal. The Church prospered and grew in number, but many looked upon her from a distance as naive, fundamentalistic, somewhat behind the times because of her popular devotions.

The Church was not inclined toward mysticism or to apparitions. When I undertook my first assignment of teaching in the U.S.A. in 1966, Fr. Cole, program director of the

Marian Library of Dayton, warned me:
— "Do not talk about apparitions. This European theme is
of no interest to the American people. It is your par-
ticularism."

I have to smile today when I quote this maxim. Now France
has become allergic to apparitions and the United States more
receptive.

Breath and Tornado of the Council

Vatican II was opened to the world, to the critics, to all
kinds of movements (good and bad), to the Bible, to
Ecumenism but also to relativism, to indifference, to psychoanalysis, even to oriental prayer techniques, which
invaded certain monasteries.

This ambiguous breath of modernism instigated renewals
and not only deviations but also disintegrations, first of all
in the clergy. The United States was one of four countries
whose priests left in record numbers. Educational classes in
psychology in all forms became the norm. Many priests and
bishops reacted against them. Homosexuality was one such
topic. This commendable concern of not discriminating
against homosexuality brought about pastoral directives
valorizing this deviance instead of providing therapeutic care.
According to a theory spread underhandedly...sexuality is
private and it is of no concern to the Church. As a result,
a sense of pity was conveyed to them, instead of conversion,
which filled them with freedom. They entered many seminaries in great numbers and were welcome with the same laxity.
These deviant vocations, without chastity, caused the authentic ones to leave, and the others to increase. What resulted
was the sexual abuse which scandalized Christian people but
was sanctioned by American law. Some bishops travel ingeni-
ously on this path by turning a deaf ear to the complaints
from the people of their dioceses. These people submit the
problems before the tribunals, and the Bishops, who are

responsible for their priests, are forced to pay heavy fines.[1] In July 1991, a newspaper reported that the Archdiocese of Washington had been forced to pay millions of dollars in fines for a homosexual priest who had been imprudently ordained after having been in three seminaries (of which one, an excellent one, turned him away).

The deviant feminists also caused chaos within the religious communities of the nuns, where the gift of oneself to service would often provide them with a platform to vent their freedom and their rights. Moreover, some even went as far as supporting the abortion movement. We do not wish to expose in detail Satan's "smoke" as Pope Paul VI identified it. Much damage was done in the North Atlantic countries.

There is also deviance within the theology faculty, opened to all without discernment, and to the culture of human sciences without reference to God. The spirit of criticism and the taste of originality at all cost, emptied theology of all contemplative dimensions and sometimes of God Himself under the influence of "too much ideology." These methods and this illusion deformed many catechists educated in those faculties.

Renewal

In this climate of superficial dispersion, theology was being reduced to human sciences, forgetting even God. The pastoral

---

FOOTNOTE

1. In 1980, I had written twice to the Bishops' Conference inquiring about what had been done as to the articles of *Sipe* and others, which manifests the start of this invasion in the Catholic Clergy by homosexuality, in the footsteps of the Episcopalians, whose clergy numbers 20% homosexuals, even though they have married clergy. They answered politely: "We ignore it."

   These trials have dragged the Church into a financial crisis more serious than they had bargained for. Their faithful reply: "We are ready to sacrifice in the name of the service of the Church but not to pay for the trials of homosexuals."

was opened to the social without the integration of an evangelical inspiration; the catechists, to the dynamic of the group, without sufficient reference even to the Faith. The very solid American Catholicism reacted, sometimes by traditionalism, but most often by an impressive return to basic roots.

Thus, the *Charismatic Renewal* was born spontaneously in 1967. The young, noble but suffocated in this socio-cultural climate of post Vatican II, were looking ardently into the new Pentecost, which John XXIII had prophesied. Briefly they had recourse to the *"Cursillo de Cristianidad,"* and later they became aware of the experience of being baptized in the Spirit through the Episcopalian's neopentecostal movement. This experience of the baptism in the Spirit is presented in the Bible like a normal complement (sometimes anticipation) to that of the Baptism of water (*Matt.* 3:11; *Lk.* 3:16; *Jn.* 1:33; *Acts* 1:5; *Acts* 11:16).

The Charismatic Renewal radiated immensely throughout the entire world, because it responded to an interior hunger and thirst for the presence, the meeting, the concrete communication with God and lastly to spiritual efficaciousness according to the number one need of the Church. But this movement is only one form and one aspect of a larger return to the essential: Prayer, gift of self and encounter with God. Certainly the Charismatic Renewal did not have the monopoly.

Prayer Groups

The same pursuit has found its way into various informal groups, classical and traditional. The Rosary is being recited, litanies, various consecrations and long-forgotten prayers since the Council. I have seen a number of these groups in the United States. One of them for example, meets regularly in New York, in the house of Conchita, the principal visionary of Garabandal, who has founded an excellent prayer group. Every week people come to pray there, in a traditional way, without ever mentioning the word apparitions. It has been such across the country. Large prayer groups were formed in many parishes. This was the case in Scottsdale.

Medjugorje

The strongest movement these past years has been the issue of Medjugorje. However, during 1984-1985 my talks on the apparitions of Medjugorje were received with much restraint and reservation. It was not until 1985 that a New York Catholic company interviewed me at length about the subject. Then, two years later there was a "rush." Chartered planes flew the 8,000 miles to the Adriatic bringing tens of thousands of pilgrims. Over a hundred "Queen of Peace" centers sprang up all over America. These centers were useful in giving out information and stimulating and coordinating thousands of prayer groups which continue to multiply to this day.

Medjugorje was instrumental in inspiring a renewal of prayer and communication with God. This was not accomplished feverishly or in an illuminism way by psychological action, but from deep within their hearts, by conversion and gift of self.

There was a religious community, "Mother of God," (near Washington) which arose from a classical prayer group in the early 1960s, and it rallied around the Charismatic Movement. It provided them with new ways of deepening their relationship with God, much before the apparitions in Medjugorje. At the time of my first visit to this community, I was staying with a pleasant family, and one of the first questions I was asked by the lady of the house at breakfast was:
—"What has the Lord said to you this morning?"

In this family it was natural to take part in the word of knowledge received during the morning prayers: not "locutions" but the inspirations and word of knowledge that God gives to all who have an open heart and are assiduous in their prayer life.

In certain parish prayer groups, and in other groups, this quest for communicating with God awakens so-called locutions. Listening to God or to Our Lady permits a distinctive response to be heard. Such was the case in Scottsdale where this phenomenon brought about some anxieties, but progressed silently thanks to the humility of the pastor and his parishioners, who obeyed most scrupulously the restrictions imposed by higher authorities.

Scottsdale

Upon returning from a pilgrimage to Medjugorje, the pastor of St. Maria Goretti, awakened to new spiritual dimensions, welcomed succesively in two stages, six then nine young parishioners who, at various degrees and under very different forms had received the gift of prayer, of healing, charisms, locutions and apparitions included.

It seems to me that the awakening of this parish falls under many exemplary titles.

1. These visionaries have experienced an authentic spiritual growth characterized by the gift of themselves, trials, sacrifices. Some have yielded to the Spiritual Dark Night and are in advanced stages of the mystical life.
2. Their charisms go hand in hand with this essential development and present, at various degrees, serious signs of authenticity.
3. They are not part of the "Charismatic Renewal." It is another movement initiated by the Holy Spirit.
4. If the influence of Medjugorje is seen as a catalyst and a place of conversion, it is not a matter of simply mimicry. The awakening of the visionaries came about from within. Medjugorje was instrumental in some of their lives but not in all of them. For some, it was Confession or inspiration that was the decisive factor. The movement, developing at its own pace, bore many fruits by way of moderation and obedience, which was not always easy.

The autonomy of this spiritual renewal has its own importance. It confirms that it is not a way, a manner or fashion, but that it rises within you, from both a profound need that God has put in the heart of man, and the gift of the Holy Spirit which is a gushing fountain from the innermost part of your being (*Jn.* 4:14). He inspires each person according to his/her own character, a sincere thirst, and He comes to respond from the interior. Thus, analogous graces surface a little everywhere. Medjugorje is but a blessed site, privileged to be the instrument of the workings of the Holy Spirit in union with Our Lady.

Often these misunderstood graces are ignored, repressed or suffocated in a cultural and social milieu where the evangelical seed is sterilized (*Matt.* 13:5-7).

On the contrary, at Scottsdale this grace found a serious and Christian environment well catechized, where it was welcomed by an exemplary pastoral support. Facing the unusual, which was expanding rapidly, Father Spaulding seemed to have found this narrow strait (passage) between Charybde and Scylla, between illuminism and repression, thanks to his being compliant, his fastidiousness and his prudent discernment and awareness not to quench the Holy Spirit (*1 Thess.* 5:9), a difficult position rarely accomplished.

He was particularly aware to channel God's working in their hearts and to avoid creating a division in the parish.

He was sensitive to the signs of the times, both earthly and celestial ones. One day he received this message: "Be merciful. You have not been merciful" (toward a particular visionary or another). This delicate event had an impact on him.

This book will attempt to be all of the following: an evocation, a discernment, an evaluation. This being understood, we shall go forward with the significant facts comprising the importance of Scottsdale in order to grasp the interior genesis and the meaning of it.

Medicine, being discerning in itself, has an interest in the history of health and sicknesses. The genesis of every human being reveals the causes, remedies and the need of each patient. Accordingly, the surprising development of Scottsdale will lead us to the messages, which are self-explanatory; to personal graces and to graces for the whole community, from whence they are born, and to the future of the movement.

Publisher's Note

The following 14 pages are pictures of the principal participants in the events at St. Maria Goretti Parish and some of the settings in which Our Lord and Our Lady make their presence known. Hopefully, this will help you to further visualize the ordinariness of these people and their parish as you read about the very unusual occurrences taking place in their individual lives and in the life of the community around them.

As Our Lord and Our Lady have not always manifested themselves to those we mortals might consider most worthy or even most receptive, it is especially unprecedented that they would work wonders in such an ordinary, reasonably affluent, American suburban area. This particular event, the key players and the apparent good fruits bear evidence that our trust must be placed in Him Who draws us to Himself. Our own inability to comprehend the ways of the Lord, in and of itself, gives glory to Him.

Fr. Laurentin and Gianna

Gianna during apparition at home

Thursday night prayer group

Mary Cook and Jimmy Kupanoff

Gianna

Jimmy, Mary, Steve, Wendy, Susan, Stefanie, Gianna and Fr. Jack

Steve and Wendy Nelson

Our Lady of Joy—"The roses are your prayers."

Stefanie Staab

James, Wendy, Mary, Annie, Fr. Jack, Gianna and Steve

Center of the Chapel

The Tabernacle Chapel

Steve Nelson in his former career

Fr. Jack and St. Maria Goretti Church

Fr. Jack and Susan Evans

*Statue of Our Lord
in St. Maria Goretti*

*Statue of Our Lady
in St. Maria Goretti*

James Pauley

Susan Evans

Annie Ross

Mary Cook

Jimmy Kupanoff

Wendy Nelson

Carol Ameche

Fr. Ernest Larkin
(Head of Commission)

CHAPTER 1

An Unexpected Success

Radiation of a Message

The American publisher of my books is The Riehle Foundation, a non-profit organization established to produce and distribute Catholic materials.

In late 1989, my friend Bill Reck, a director of the Riehle Foundation, sent to me the manuscript of a book they were in the process of publishing. The book was titled: *I Am Your Jesus of Mercy*, and contained the messages and lessons from Our Lord and Our Lady allegedly being received by several young people at St. Maria Goretti Parish in Scottsdale, Arizona.

Bill and Fran Reck had spent much time in prayer and discernment over these messages and, deeply impressed with their content, had agreed to take on the sole responsibility of publishing them in a low cost, not-for-profit book.

Should It be Published?

I daily receive a great amount of messages from all over the world. It is quite impossible to read all of them. Besides, my sensitiveness has diminished. I am like an apprentice in a pastry shop where the owner has given him permission to eat as many cakes as he wishes until he no longer has the taste for them. Prudence and criticism do not always sharpen one's spiritual sensitivity.

My answer to Bill Reck was not encouraging.

After quickly researching them, I said simply: "All this is irreproachable. The messages which originated in that

1

parish are meant for that parish. They bring about the stimulation of many fruits, but are they meant to be preserved? Does this local patrimony have universal importance? It is not evident. Every site of apparitions tend to think they are another Lourdes or a new Fatima destined to enlighten the world, and so they over-react to the importance of their messages. The increase of all these phenomena seems to indicate a decentralization, making them commonplace, which calls for discernment."

Being more sensitive than I was as to Christian opinions and its needs, Bill Reck was able to perceive justly. However modestly presented, this book was a huge success. By 1991, 2 years later, over 150,000 copies were distributed. The 2nd Volume, published in August 1990 already had passed 100,000 copies at the time of my investigation of Scottsdale in July 1991. The 3rd volume came out in September 1991 with a first printing of 40,000. Success is always revealing. The books responded to the hunger and the spiritual thirst of the people as did the messages of Medjugorje, which the intellectuals deplore because of its banality but the Christian masses accept like words of life that nourish and convert them.

Value of the Messages—Holiness

What need do these messages fulfill and how come they are so well received? They are perceived as a source from which spiritual life emerges, and many have such a need in a demanding and materialistic world, and in a Church where life is suffocated by ideology and abstraction. Many Christians are tired of a cerebral theology, a moralizing pastorship, which is activist, focusing more on the social aspect without inspiration or light. People are desperately searching for a contact with God, His love and His presence. They are concerned with meeting Him and communicating effectively with Him in faith's dark night but not one without stars. This is exactly what the St. Maria Goretti prayer groups advocate so well.

There, the classical prayer of the rosary is recited slowly

in the light of the Joyful, Sorrowful and Glorious Mysteries. This prayer effectively opened the heart of the faithful to the call from Heaven of September 20, 1988, revealing its lively communication with this community.

This first lesson in the messages book was received unexpectedly by a young parishioner—it was a call to holiness. This visionary (Gianna Talone) remained anonymous for a long time. This message consisted of three sentences:

> *My child, I would like you to start being and living the holiness of Me...not only in your actions but also in your daily thoughts and feelings. Do not be holy only superficially, be holy within and throughout your entire body. Be Me.*

Gianna says it was Jesus speaking—an echo from a well-known biblical text:

> *Be Holy, for I, Yahweh your God, am Holy* (*Lev.* 19:2; 20:26). *Be perfect like your Father is perfect* (insists Jesus in *Matt.* 5:48).

On the Side of Psychology

This message brings us back to the side of psychology (whose concern today is mostly, if not totally, to *existence*). God's existence, affirmed by the Scriptures, is the holiness of the Supreme Being. It is through Him that the Christians can find their identity—this famous "identity" of which we are speaking. To be more specific, they can find it only in Jesus Christ: God made man who has made of us one living being only, one body only—kin to the words of St. Paul: (*Phil.* 1:21)—"Life to me, of course, is Christ, but then death would be a positive gain."

This does not mean the annihilation or extinction of one's personality. On the contrary, the visionaries are a living proof. To identify one's self with Divine Love is neither absorption nor indistinct fusion. It allows the best possibilities for individuals to blossom according to their diversity and their creativity, in oneness that Love achieves similar to that of the model of the transcending Trinity. There the absolute identity of the Supreme Being does not extinguish the existence and the communication of the Persons, but creates it.

An ex-Christian, completely taken by psycho-analysis and psychology, was bragging about the success of his profession in resolving the problem of death: "It is possible to obtain a peaceful death if we are able to recall a happy moment, the best possible moment of our existence, and recall this happy moment at the time of death and this calms anxiety." Maybe, but life and death...and God, are beyond the superficial subjective balms. It is the same with today's medicine which encourages women to have abortions and then gives them sedatives or psychotherapy. It would be better to avoid the destructive acts which generate anxiety.

The Source

The first message of Scottsdale asks for holiness but most of all presents its source: God Himself. He invites us to identify with Him. It is in this profound identity in the Body of Jesus Christ that all our being is able to be sanctified. It is God's doing, Jesus Christ, but He does nothing within us without us. This first message sets the tone. It has a founding mission.

That very day on which this lesson was received came a commentary on the Sorrowful Mysteries, the forgotten summit of Jesus Christ's work on earth. His Passion is His supreme glory according to the fourth Gospel. It is the proof and the efficacious moment of His love. This preliminary message was an invitation to the compassion and participation in the Passion of Our Lord. At the same time, it serves as an invitation to abolish all fear, and this also responds to the needs of many. The messages are a prayerful catechesis: both doctrinal and moral. But the doctrine is not all abstract, it is personalized. The moral is not moralism but dynamism. It is not in words but spirit. It is not a law, but a grace.

All is centered on the living presence of God who is talking to hearts (*Hosea* 2:16). He speaks of love, life and the gift of self. He invites us to acts of grace, to prayer, to fasting. There is equilibrium between mysticism and asceticism, love and confidence. He leads us to love on a road paved with trials.

Everything stems from the Trinity itself. Christ gives back to His Father and gives us the Holy Spirit. In short, these messages contain a doctrinal content, and they propose a doctrine in an existential way, like an encounter, a contemplation and the source of life. It is at the same time a modern and authentic presentation of Christian revelation, which is not abstract, but an invitation to life. The messages are given not to individuals, but to a large community of prayer.

They manifest the quality, the transparency, and the equilibrium of this prayer. The locutions from Our Lady and Our Lord both emerge and respond. They stimulate and invigorate.

Contemplation of Christ in the Spirit leads to the Father and to the Trinity entirely. It abounds with a spiritual engagement. The titles which summarize each lesson in the books express them very well: "Sincerity," "Conversion," "Simplicity," "Confidence," "Faith," "Charity," "Unity" (ecumenism), "Gift of the Heart," etc...

Our Lord and Our Lady

The quoted messages at Scottsdale are Theocentric and Christocentric (even more clearly than the ones of Medjugorje): 80% are lessons attributed to Our Lord and 20% only to Our Lady (a little more perhaps in the 3rd volume of messages).

Our Lady's messages are well situated. They preceed those of Our Lord by 2 months, and were in preparation for the 1st lesson message from Jesus (September 20, 1988). The first message from Our Lady was July 14, 1988:

> *My children, open your hearts to Jesus: He wants to fill you with His grace. He wants to give you His joy, and He wants your joy to be complete..."*

The messages of Our Lady are maternal, insinuating. They stimulate confidence and prayer. They guide by beauty toward truth and right.

> *My dear children, if only you knew how beautiful you are when you pray. Much glory is given Jesus when your prayer is from the heart...* (August 4, 1988).
> *Please pray. You are so beautiful, my dear children, when you pray...* (August 5, 1988).
> *My dear children, ...you are so beautiful; beautiful like a growing flower and Jesus is your vine* (September 14, 1988).

The message is not a hodge-podge of whatsoever. It is different than the one from Medjugorje or anywhere else in language, tone, themes. It is an inspiration, a reflection of the American religious culture which does not separate contemplation, psychology, and realistic ·engagement.

The publisher gave a spontaneous priority to the messages of Christ (regardless of the chronological order).

These messages have played a specific role in the parish according to a pedagogical progression. Having been received orally, they somehow lose some dynamic and vivid value once they were compiled in a volume. But nevertheless, the significant success of the books tend to prove that their value lingers and nourishes.

Thus went I to Scottsdale in order to understand.

CHAPTER 2

On The Way To Scottsdale

The Megapolis—Oasis of Phoenix in the Desert of Arizona

Here I am on the freeway from Los Angeles to Phoenix, the capital of Arizona. The population of the state is something over two million people. The climate changes fast as we are making our way eastward from the fresh greenery near the Pacific Ocean, to the torrid and sandy plains area, one of the most arid regions in the States. The vast plains are set against a chain of small mountains, somber in color, sculptured in angular relief.

Midway in passing, near the Colorado River, the frontier between California and Arizona, we find sporadically here and there a few dwellings (adobe), somewhat makeshift, and some vegetation along the river.

Then the plains whither away and become desert. But along the way greenery reappears, sumptuously in the cultivated parts of this immense oasis, due to dams located in the distance and irrigation-water projects around Phoenix. Greenery is evident and cannot be overlooked anywhere, neither in the fields nor in the streets where trees are planted throughout the city. Is this symbolic of Saint Maria Goretti Parish, a living source in the desert of materialistic surroundings?

We arrive in Scottsdale, 100,000 plus inhabitants, a portion of the Phoenix metropolis (similar to Versailles for Paris). And here is the well-built parish, about 20 years old, in an impeccable suburb area of Phoenix.

7

At the right stands the church, a structure which has two large arches made of concrete. To the left is the parish office and meeting rooms. After making our way across a vast lawn, green despite the heat, we are welcomed by a smiling secretary, Marge Perry. Everything breathes order and harmonious activity, Phoenix style.

The megapolis originated from an extensive undertaking (land development) in the West at the beginning of the century. Dams were built on the Salt River (1911) and on the Gila (1928). Thus arose culture and cities within the framework of diversification planned in Washington by Roosevelt.

This agricultural development also ultimately became an industrial food center, including meats and textiles, then an economic metropolis that provided both electronic and aeronautical equipment, thanks to the importance of its strategic and climatic location. It is also a retirement area. The suburb called Sun City was built largely for senior citizens. A younger atmosphere characterizes Saint Maria Goretti Parish due to its youth.

There are 2,600 families in the parish (about 6,000 persons). It is well organized by the pastor. In order to be more free to attend to spiritual needs, he has confided the administration to Sandra Bruner, like St. Peter had discharged his service ("service of the tables") to the seven. All the activity sectors are guided by competent persons: Bible studies, music, welcoming committees, etc.

The secretary introduced us to Fr. Jack Spaulding in his office, which is warm and impeccably furnished.

CHAPTER 3

The Pastor of Saint Maria Goretti

I had no previous knowledge of Fr. Jack Spaulding. He is quite the opposite from many other American pastors in temperament and physique. He, by contrast, is thin and slight, in his 40s, has an aquiline nose and sharp gaze. His demeanor is relaxed which is typical of very busy men. Beset on all sides, Fr. Jack Spaulding remains smiling and hospitable which is incredible in such a busy and lively parish.

The Deaf-mutes

I asked many questions about his curriculum because, as it is in all things, the genesis is the key to the present and to the future. He answered in a friendly manner, unaffectedly and unperplexed.

He was born at the end of the Second World War and ordained to the priesthood on June 5, 1971. He was given the pastoral care of the handicapped. This he handled with aplomb, confidence and social grace along with his gift of adaptability. He has learned to talk with the hands, the sign language of the deaf-mutes. At the end of two years of study, he was able to translate any speech in sign language. Also, he is able to celebrate Mass in sign language—hands and arms able to speak at the same time as the voice, inaudible for his parishioners. He still can celebrate Mass in this silent language. Fr. Jack has been able to penetrate through the wall of deafness like an airplane is able to pierce through the sound barrier. He was thus able to bring communication to those who were unable to communicate.

9

Chancellor

At the end of nine years, on August 14, 1980, he was appointed Chancellor: that is to say, he was responsible for all the administration of the diocese. This is a prestigious task requiring competence and organization. Armed with these skills, he was able to shoulder the weight of administrative duties. He was Chancellor at the time John Paul II was traveling in the far West and the Pope visited his Chancellery.

Pastor

On November 15, 1982, he was appointed pastor of Saint Maria Goretti Parish in Scottsdale. Awaiting him was a heavy administrative task which he was able to delegate to competent personnel.

The parish had a long-standing devotion to the Eucharist, a distinct and solid foundation. This spiritual momentum was aroused by Fr. Spaulding. It was he who had a chapel built between the church and the parish office. In this intimate and quiet chapel, adoration is continuous. The Holy Sacrament is enthroned in the center protected by unbreakable glass. 700 parishioners committed themselves to perpetual adoration.

It was through the prayer groups, which began in late 1987 after his pilgrimage to Medjugorje, that the current charisms were born. The prayer groups are classical in nature, not charismatic, and the charisms were able to develop through this perfectly organized framework, where the faithful and the church are well attended to in an air-conditioned building. But here we notice it is the *spiritual* that leads rather than the material.

Besides being pastor of his parish, Fr. Jack, confident and close to the youth, is also on the Board of Directors of St. John's Seminary in Camarillo, California, representing the Diocese of Phoenix. As a member of this board, he traveled a great deal, even as far as Los Angeles.

He arrived at Saint Maria Goretti as a capable, serious, active priest. But like most, he was in search of a personal and pastoral awakening in the "traverse of the desert" of post-Vatican II. Like many he had a thirst and hunger for God, for himself and his parishioners, but was not able to totally ignite this light which forms the awakening flame that embraces in accordance with the invitation of Jesus Christ:

I have come to bring fire to the earth, and how
I wish it were blazing already! (Lk. 12:49).

He does not lack initiative. At the beginning of 1987 his communication skills enabled him to organize a "Life Teen Television Program" (ages 13-19) with Fr. Dale Fushek on Mother Angelica's EWTN ("Eternal Word Television Network").

A Report on Medjugorje—June 25, 1987

It was this television program that led him to Medjugorje for the sixth anniversary of the first apparition. It was to become a new grace in his prayer life and a spiritual awakening.

He came equipped with cameras and assorted technical aids. But this adventure (a crossing of the Red Sea—as he calls it) was for him a spiritual event.

— "During this pilgrimage I realized how much Jesus and Mary love us. They invite us to come closer to them. Upon my return I prayed a lot."

It was at this time that the people of Arizona became inflamed with Medjugorje. When Fr. Jack envisioned his television trip, he had already forseen a pilgrimage for his parishioners for October 1987. He thus returned in the fall with his parishioners: youth and adults (it was this second pilgrimage that brought Jimmy Kupanoff and Mary Cook...Mary's confession there with Fr. Pavich changed her life). It proved to be a profound experience for all.

Medjugorje had become for them a spiritual source. Fr. Jack returned three times in 1988, in March, at the beginning of June, and in August for the closing of the Marian Year, and then a last trip in August 1989. After this he became absorbed in the parish affairs, and the influence of Medjugorje was so alive that he felt no need to return.

First Visit to the Pastor

In the fall of 1987, a parishioner came to see him. Her name is Susan Evans. She is nearly 30 years old. She is well educated and a graduate of the University of Arizona. But she does not enjoy good health and so she is unable to work in her profession. She suffers a loss of hearing and seasonal allergies which force her to travel to and from Arizona and St. Louis, Missouri, her parents' hometown. Her trials were made known to her a long time ago by the discreet presence of Jesus, who has always sustained her in her life-long trials.

The Group of Six

Susan's visit to Fr. Spaulding to relate certain supernatural manifestations was the first of many to come, from which we will see an emergence of the group of six, and then of nine, and also an unfolding of events.

—"The genesis of these meetings are important for discernment," I said to Fr. Spaulding. "Can you be precise in giving me the exact dates!"

—"But all this happened day by day. I did not keep a record," he replied.

At my insistence, he reflected and later during another interview he said:

—"Instead of dates, I was able to reconstruct the order of these contacts. Here they are in order with the approximate dates inasmuch as we could reconstruct them."

In order to better understand the list that he established, we need to bear in mind Gianna's premonitory vision dated July 14, 1988. On that day she saw the group of nine (including herself) who were to be involved in these events and recognized each as they eventually came forward to Fr. Jack.

In her vision, one of them, Jimmy, left and James Pauley came into the group. Then Jimmy came back. As to Stefanie, she was standing apart from the group in the vision. This would be indicative of her role apart from the others and in accordance with a message received by Stefanie. As for Annie (number 9), she was seen less clearly by Gianna in a manner that did not identify her with the others.

There is a minor problem of numeration in the list that follows as presented by Fr. Jack. Stefanie is presented chronologically as the second one as per contact with Susan and Fr. Spaulding. It seemed logical to give her the number two, but she specifies that she was not added to the group initially but is the seventh one to come forward.

The order is as follows:

1. Susan Evans (here the first visit of Stefanie Staab, No. 7)
2. Gianna Talone (June '88)
3. Mary Cook
4. Steve Nelson
5. Wendy Nelson
6. Jimmy Kupanoff
7. Stefanie Staab
8. James Pauley
9. Annie Ross
10. Father Jack Spaulding is not only the pastor but the official guide. He belongs interiorly in this special group because he often receives messages at the very time of his homilies, since February 25, 1989, at the Thursday evening Mass.

This list was useful in conducting the initial investigation which will be the subject of the following chapter.

CHAPTER 4

Genesis of the Scottsdale Group

Let us become acquainted with the nine young people (16 to 30 years old in 1987), who successively contacted Father Jack Spaulding to confide their unusual experiences which were occurring. We will present them in the same order in which they came to the pastor, from autumn of 1987 to springtime of 1989.

I interviewed them in Scottsdale at the end of July and the beginning of August 1991.

1. Susan Evans

Susan (born January 22, 1958), single, is a graduate of the University of Arizona with a Business and Marketing Major; she has been ill since the age of 11.

She was very pious in her youth and received rare visions of Our Lord. She was barely able to realize the impact of His words to her: *You will lead many people to Me.*

She would pray often and would cry while making the Way of the Cross. As years went by, her fervor diminished as she was consumed by the time spent on her studies, her goals and her ill health.

She stated: "During that period, I would go to Mass only from time to time, on Sundays three times out of six. I felt unworthy of Our Lord and did not dare go to Confession. The estrangement grew. In the autumn of 1987, I had not been to church for seven months. I believe to have heard this invitation: *Pray to the Blessed Mother.*

"This seemed to be coming from Our Lord. Later I heard this request: *Would you suffer for me?*

14

"It was in a different atmosphere and upon the acceptance of this request that another followed: *Would you suffer for others?*

"Following this," she continued, "I finally went to see Father Spaulding in the autumn of 1987. He explained to me the positive side of my experience, in reference to Medjugorje where he had just returned from his first trip. I said to him: 'Why Medjugorje instead of this parish?'

"The Blessed Mother had told me long ago that she would come. I was 11 years old at that time. I thought she meant here."

After this first visit to Father Spaulding she received a new blessing—an awareness of Our Lord which previously had been somewhat obscure.

"He was already within me but I could not distinguish whether it was reality or a dream. I would see Him interiorly, dressed in a white robe and saying to me: *You will bring many people to Me.*

"One Saturday," continues Susan, "during the five o'clock Mass, I heard Father Spaulding preaching. I had a locution: *Go to Confession to Father Jack!*

"I went with fear, but since then my fear of Confession has disappeared. Ever since, I have been going to Mass daily. After Mass, I would pray for a long time, one or two hours. The Blessed Virgin invited me to help form a prayer group for young adults.

"I protested: 'But I am sick and unable.' She answered: *Pray, trust in Me.*

"Six months later, I protested: 'How can I continue with my health problems?' She re-iterated: *Pray, trust in Me!*

"I did have trust and now I help the young people to unite, to come together to pray, to come to church, to make friends. The prayer group now numbers 50 to 70 young people. I am sustained and helped by receiving interior locutions since 1987. Our Blessed Mother led me to know that I would be part of the six who came together in September 1988.

"My first daily prayer is to pray to God in giving Him thanks."

Father Jack remembers this first meeting:
"She had been the first one to confide in me about her graces (blessings): locutions since 1987. She came back in September 1988 when the sharing among the nine started."

She plays an intimate role, discreet and fruitful within the group. Her life runs parallel to the Suffering Servant in *Isaiah* 53, corresponding to a long line of victims during the eras of the 17th to the 19th centuries, more distinctively than in our time as it were. Similar to Vicka (Medjugorje) she is going through some illnesses (known as Lupus, fibromyalgia, and scleroderma) and other unexplainable, disconcerting health problems. "The Lord is my Mediator," she says. Spiritual trials followed. God's ways are not our ways. His way is by virtue of His Cross which has a place in the progression of events in Scottsdale.

Susan has been called to total abandonment of self in solidarity with suffering people and sinners. She prays; she counsels effectively without gossiping. Her influence is beyond words. She plays an interior and unobtrusive role within the group. And she bears its burden interiorly: "I offer my sufferings for the young people of the entire world," she said.

She pursues a remarkable spiritual ascension, in a walled-in world due to her partial deafness, by total giving of herself. She has been blessed with a conversation with Our Lord and Our Lady and a fruitful charism for the foundation of the young adult prayer group. The grace in which she lives is communicated thusly by conversion and abandonment to God. Her only concern is that of guiding others to God. Jesus has given her the symbolic name of *"Charity,"* in conformity with her vocation.

Stefanie Staab

It was in 1987 that Stefanie Staab realized her conversion and launched the first prayer groups in the parish jointly with

Fr. Spaulding. Stefanie was absent at the time of my trip to Scottsdale. I had her interviewed by Doris Laguette and Bill Reck.

When describing Stefanie all witnesses talk about her enthusiastically, in eloquent terms.

She is an accomplished, pretty, likable and self-confident young woman. Without a doubt, she deserves her symbolic name of *Joy*. Her role will be that of emissary of Scottsdale. "What a fitting role in view of the gifts bestowed upon her," writes Doris Laguette—(my translator).

Bill Reck goes beyond the above comments by stating she is joyous, intelligent and attractive.

"A very brilliant young lady," says Fr. Jack (who places their first meeting as June of 1988, at the time of his third pilgrimage to Medjugorje, apparently overlooking the initial contact which occurred in autumn of 1987).

One of the visionaries (Gianna) related the following detailed account of her remarkable personality:

"Her intelligence is analytical but sometimes too critical. She is resilient and endowed with a very caring attitude (paternal) toward others. She is optimistic and a perfectionist." She is spiritually guided by Fr. F.

She was born in West Hempstead, Long Island, New York, on September 2, 1962. She enjoys sports, namely skiing, camping and target shooting.

She graduated from the University of Arizona in 1987 (finance and accounting) and held a high-level position in management which was accompanied by a very good salary. At that time, she was not very pious. She had been raised in a Catholic home but her parents had been divorced since she was five years old. This was not conducive to her formation. She felt more or less like a "forced Catholic" and her faith was only routine.

At the age of 25, in 1987, a friend at Stefanie's place of employment had a conversion. Stefanie felt a deep respect for her sincerity and the courage with which she was able to cope in regard to her Faith and her profession. She then started to take stock of herself, about her responsibilities toward God and toward others.

During the summer of 1987, she saw Fr. Jack Spaulding's video on Medjugorje, *The Life Teen Program.* She then met Susan Evans. She felt compelled to say to Susan: "I need to talk with you." "I know," said Susan.

Both had the same intuition that Our Lady would visit the parish. They started the young adult prayer group that meets on Friday. Steve and Wendy Nelson and Mary Cook joined them. Many young people came and were converted.

It was while attending this prayer group that she met Fr. Spaulding, who in turn approved the formation of the Thursday night prayer group. A short time later (August 1988) she came to tell him:

"I think I'm going crazy. I hear a voice which urges me to write something for the conversion of the parish."

"I helped her discern that it possibly was the voice of the Blessed Mother," Fr. Spaulding explained. Stefanie felt a need to write. "It is not me," she stated, "and I do not understand what is happening to me."

One day in church, she felt a tingling sensation in her ear accompanied by an intense interior feeling. She decided to write and states she had no control over her writing. She wanted to express one thing and would write something else totally different.

She heard about Gianna's locutions and asked her, "What happens when you have a locution?" She understood that the same thing was happening to her, however, with a different modality. That very day, she received a special locution from Our Lady and started to receive messages every evening at home upon returning from work.

"These messages are slightly different from those of Gianna," explained Father Spaulding. "At the beginning they were actual teachings. She would report them to me saying, 'The voice tells me this and I do not understand.' After having read them, I saw that she could not have known what they meant. They concerned conversion of the heart. It was a beautiful teaching, theological as well as pastoral, convergent with those of Gianna. I said to Stefanie: 'Just listen, that's all.' "

Since then she dedicates more time to prayer, with a special intention for the young people of the parish. She writes the information and the messages which she hands over regularly to Fr. Jack.

The messages from Our Lord started in the summer of 1988. A trial was soon to follow. In October, her health deteriorated. She contracted mononucleosis, diagnosed as having started from chronic fatigue syndrome (known as Epstein Barr syndrome). She experienced a serious relapse in 1989. She was forced to stop working full-time for nine months (except for a few consulting assignments). These months proved to be uncertain (precarious), but invaluable. It was during this sabbatical period that Our Lady molded her in a profound way with the help of her spiritual director.

Stefanie changed her residence and went to live with five other young women who shared the same spiritual interests. She had thoughts of starting a religious community, but it did not materialize. Nothing seemed to go right. Always sick, she was unable to work. In the fall of 1990 she found a good job in Dallas, but returned to Scottsdale, sensing she had to be there. She found work but on a lower scale, in contrast with the prestigious job she had held previously. This job was that of a file clerk. After having been on a management level, it was a humbling experience. But this humiliation was beneficial to Stefanie, and Jesus explained to her the significance of this trial as being a formative period.

She states that Our Lady asked her if she would be willing to suffer, and in turn, Our Lady promised her that she would appear to her occasionally, as need be. She receives private messages which have never been published. She was not asked to publish them.

It was in 1988 that she became aware of others in the parish who were receiving messages and locutions. She also understood that Susan Evans has an undefined role in the events in progress, and she was aware of the breadth of her sufferings.

In 1987, while praying in Church late at night, Stefanie had a vision of Satan—grotesque and terrifying in appearance. Steve Nelson's experience of Satan was similar to this. She often senses this presence from "down under." She was told that Satan appears visibly when all else has failed. And so he does this as a last resort to frighten.

It was in December 1988 that she was added to the group of visionaries with Annie and James Pauley (but Fr. Spaulding lists Annie's name as the last one).

Stefanie has become a Eucharistic Minister in the parish and participates in the Thursday and Friday night prayer groups. She considers herself to be the first of the three added to the original group of six. She continues to radiate her symbol: *Joy.*

2. Gianna Talone

The third person that the Holy Spirit "awakened" in the spiritual movement in Scottsdale is Gianna Talone. She is a young woman, brunette, possessing high intelligence and sensitivity—this finesse being typical of her Italian origin. Being a Pharm. Dr. (clinical pharmacist), she is in charge of the geriatric pharmaceutical section of St. Joseph Hospital in Phoenix. She turned 35 years old on March 12, 1992. She had been married to a graphic designer.

Before her pilgrimage to Medjugorje, she had a modest and personal spiritual experience:

"It was in September 1987," Gianna told me, "I awakened from sleep and was quite conscious that I had seen Our Blessed Mother in front of me, a little to the right—a young, slender woman dressed in a light white dress and veil."

I asked her, "It was during the night, at what time?"

Gianna answered, "I do not remember. I was surprised. I asked myself who it was. I was awakened thusly three nights in a row. I would look at the Blessed Virgin and she would look at me. She did not talk but I felt a great peace in my heart—evidence that it was not a dream. I was sure of that. After this, I experienced a great hunger for the Eucharist. I would go to Mass daily; I would pray long hours. I could hardly pull myself away from praying.

"In November 1987, one day while in church, I tried to get up after praying and I could not. I heard an interior voice; this voice came from the heart and entered in my prayer. This voice came from behind me. While I could not identify it, it gave me great peace. I was wishing to remain in this state. The voice told me: *The Lord seeks favor upon you for you have cried for the Lord. He wants to do great things through you.* I found out later that it had been the voice of Angel Gabriel."

Medjugorje: June 1988

"In June 1988, Fr. Jack was going to Medjugorje with a group. I could not go because of a medical convention. All of a sudden, the convention was cancelled and I was able to go. I was able to obtain the last available seat on the plane going to Medjugorje."

Shortly after their arrival on the third of June, Gianna met Wayne Weible, a Lutheran journalist, who consecrated his life to Medjugorje. He was giving a talk. Gianna and her mother were in the audience, and since all the seats were taken, she was standing on the side, against the wall. Wayne glanced to that side and his eyes rested on her. Later he confided that he had seen her surrounded with a halo of light.

At the end of his presentation, as he was mingling with the audience, he was led to tell her, "You will play a very significant role in Our Blessed Mother's plan." Gianna looked at him as if he were crazy.

"Here is a man who is unbalanced!" she thought. She relates the following:

"The next day as I was making the Way of the Cross, climbing Mt. Krizevac, I heard: *Pray for peace and I will bless you.* I recognized the voice to be that of the Blessed Virgin. She was talking to me for the first time. Since then, she talks to me every day. At the same time, I had a vision

of a crucifix and I understood that I had to go in front of
the Cross and pray for peace for nations, for families and
for our souls.

"On that very same day I saw a crucifix in the parish book-
store. It was the same as the one in my vision on Mt.
Krizevac. The colors were the same: brown cross, white
corpus, eyes opened. I mentioned it to Fr. Spaulding, whom
I hardly knew at the time. His response was so indifferent,
like he did not want to pursue it further. 'That's nice.' I did
not pursue it.

"On the 6th of June as I was climbing Apparition Hill,
Our Lady's voice insisted: *Pray for peace!* 'But over here
everyone is praying,' I answered. *Yes, but people only pray
when things go wrong and they do not pray with their hearts,*
she retorted.

"I then saw Infant Jesus. He had blond, curly hair and
round cheeks and was wearing a white dress (robe) and a
small cap on His head.

"I believe that when Jesus presents Himself as a child, it
is a sign of His joy. We should all become childlike. Like
St. Peter represents the father of all generations, Jesus is the
child of all generations, because no one can enter into the
Kingdom unless they are like a child. That is what Our Lady
told me.

"At this moment, I started to doubt: Am I going crazy?
That night, upon retiring, Our Lady came into my room and
said: *My dear child, why do you doubt? Tomorrow you will
go to see Vicka and she will confirm my messages.*

"I did not see Our Lady, but my eyes were staring at a
certain place in my room and I knew she was there. I did
not answer because I was thinking: I am going crazy. But
I knew that if it were true, I would see Vicka and something
would come out of this, like Our Lady had indicated. Thus,
I remained silent.

"On the 8th of June, I walked to Vicka's house. A lot of
people were there, but as I was making my way, people were
allowing me to go through by moving to the side. Without

any shoving or pushing, I walked up to Vicka, who was standing on the steps of the stairway outside her house.

"Vicka asked me: 'What do you want?'

"I said: 'Our Lady sent me to you.'

"Vicka went up the stairs, then came back down and looked directly in my eyes. This seemed like an eternity. She said, 'I want to talk to you in private. Let me know when you can get an interpreter.'

"The next day I met Vicka in her bedroom on the second floor. She said to me: 'Keep an open heart.'

"I did not understand. After that, she would always wave to me whenever I would see her or if I went to her house. Our Lady continued to talk to me during the rest of the pilgrimage. On the last day, I met Wayne Weible in church, and I asked him if he remembered me and what he had said to me.

— " 'Yes,' he answered. I said, 'Our Lady talked to me.'

— " 'I'm very happy,' he answered, and he hugged me. But I had feelings that in his mind he was asking himself if he had created this whole thing.

— "Before our departure from Medjugorje, as I was praying in front of the statue of Our Lady in St. James Church, Our Blessed Mother spoke to me." Gianna reported this message:

— *I am going home with you, to your home. Once you were like a lost lamb and now you are found. You will do great things and many will come to you. It is time for the mission to begin. Do not worry, I am with you. I will guide you and protect you. Everything will be for the glory of God.*

"I did not talk about these events to any of the people from our pilgrimage group because I did not want them to think I was odd. I carefully mentioned it to Carol Ameche, who barely responded. I did not persist. Only my mother was supportive.

"Father Jack Spaulding was with a friend, who later became his doctor, and so during the pilgrimage, I hardly saw him except at the time of the Mass and when the group met.

"It was a week later after I had returned home, that Our Lady sent me to Fr. Spaulding.

"The following month, on July 14, 1988, I was praying my Rosary in front of the cross when I noticed a lit candle in the form of a cross. Shortly after, the Blessed Virgin sent me to Fr. Spaulding and I told him, 'I saw a vision of nine young people praying in front of the Blessed Virgin in church.' "

Gianna states she clearly and distinctly saw the seven young persons destined to receive visions and locutions (herself included). She would recognize them as each one would present themselves to the pastor. The two others she saw less clearly.

First Messages (July 1988)

It was on the same day, July 14, 1988, that Gianna received the first public message from Our Blessed Mother (Vol. 1, page 109 of the message book).

Laurentin: It was not the first time?

Gianna: I had had apparitions during the night. But I had some doubts. Since then I am more sure it was her because I recognized her. (This was the first public message.)

Laurentin: Can you describe her?

Gianna: She is so beautiful that all descriptions would be inadequate.

Laurentin: However, what can you say?

Gianna: She is young and slender with long, thin fingers, dark hair, gray-blue eyes (more bluish than gray), fair complexion, rosy cheeks and a small chin. She was wearing a white dress and light veil. The dress had no belt or ornament except gold embroidery at the collar. She was not wearing any jewelry.

Laurentin: Was it an interior or exterior vision?

Gianna: I see her as a living person.

Laurentin: Have you ever touched her?

Gianna: She kissed me on July 4, 1991...and another

time. I asked her: "Why are you so beautiful?" She answered: *Because I love.*

This brings an objection on my part. I ask:

Laurentin: Jelena had asked the very same question and she received the same answer in Medjugorje. Did you know? She appeared surprised. She was unaware of it.

Laurentin: And, after that?

Gianna: On August 10, 1988, Our Lord started to talk to me. He told me particularly, *I ask love, mercy, compassion, dignity, respect, honesty.* I received some secrets given by Our Lord to be revealed in time.

Laurentin: In other words, it is of interest to the whole world.

Gianna: There will be a sign here as in other parts of the world.

She then adds, "I asked, 'Why me? I am not any more than others?' He (Jesus) answered: *My Father has created souls where mercy will pierce. Your soul has been created for this mission of mercy. This is the age of My Divine Mercy.*

"On September 20, 1988, Our Lord started to dictate lessons to me. On December 28, 1988, I was privileged to see an apparition of Our Lord as the Sacred Heart. He is indescribably beautiful. Rays of light emanated from His Heart—they were blinding. On this day, He asked me to step down from the position I held at the pharmacy. This was costly for me. But as a result, a short time later I was able to obtain this position that I now hold—Pharmacy Coordinator of the Long Term Care Facility at St. Joseph's Hospital."

Gianna states a second apparition of Our Lord occurred on April 7, 1989.

Laurentin: Can you describe Our Lord?

This question embarrassed her like the previous one because Jesus is indescribable. She formulates as well as she can what she is going to say.

Gianna: He has brown eyes that pull you into eternity, brown hair and beard, wavy-Jewish type, tan complexion, and a white garment. His Heart was visible, projecting gold and white rays.

On this question she explains, "The heart is not character-ized by a two dimensional image. Jesus wears a gold sash. Before disappearing, He opened His hands and said: *I am your Jesus of Mercy* (referenced on page 104, Volume I of the message books).

Laurentin: Jesus has given each one of you a symbol, what is yours?

Gianna: Divine Mercy, and I would also add, *love.*

This name which she has received summarizes all the mes-sages of Scottsdale: tenderness, mercy, love given from the human heart and the divine heart of Jesus—an invitation for a new attitude in us. It is a profound inspiration of this entire spiritual movement.

It has become the title of the publication of the messages: *I Am Your Jesus of Mercy.* The word *mercy* signifies compre-hension, kindness, opening of the heart, forgiveness; an hospitable attitude toward others, one which is open and pro-found. Meanwhile, Gianna has lost former friends. They left her. They live in another world, a superficial world.

In early 1991, her husband divorced her. The Church annulled the marriage. Gianna was deeply affected by the loss of this loved one, who did not want children and could not accept the new developments in her life.

Laurentin: Concerning the devil, do you have problems, some temptations?

Gianna: Yes, I have seen Satan once. My life is not the same anymore. I suffer interiorly. But Jesus loves us so much, and we do not respond as we should.

Upon interrogating her about other trials, she simply says the following, with discretion:

Gianna: I am weak, human. I have a hard time living according to the dictates of Jesus. I fall but I pray. I try. He is teaching me to give of myself and my time to others. He is so peaceful. I love Him so much, Him and His Mother. Sometimes the Lord asks me to suffer to alleviate the wrong.

Laurentin: What kind of suffering?

Gianna: It is difficult to express how—suffering is to remain silent.

She talks somewhat like Vicka did at the time of her suffering in Medjugorje. For her, this trial might include the form of interior stigmatas.

Gianna says that Jesus also told her: *We must love. Prayers can prevent wars and cataclysm.*

Gianna is prudent, she fears illusion, because Satan can disguise himself sometimes as an angel of light. To assure herself of the identity of Our Lady she asks her, "When you come to see me, say: 'Blessed be God'...so that I can be sure it is you."

There are in fact some formulas that cannot be verbalized by Satan, had it been an effigy. She claims she has received some secrets from Our Lord and Our Lady concerning the future of the world and of the Church, the latest on August 8, 1991 (this message was from Our Lady). They were confided to her in strict confidence.

She claims three types of supernatural communications:
1. Apparitions of Jesus and Mary as living persons, present and tangible.
2. Spiritual communications (intuitive, immediate knowledge, independent of time). Gianna states she was told that it is the purest way (manner).
3. Interior locutions (hearing their voices).

During her sleep, she feels overwhelmed with other people's trials. She takes over anxieties and difficulties of persons who need assistance. Upon awakening in the morning she is completely exhausted. She experiences different charisms, especially healing, and is often asked by people for this.

3. Mary Cook

"The third young adult who contacted me was Mary Cook," says Fr. Jack.

She was a waitress at the time, having had to abandon her studies at the University after one year. She teaches young children ages 3 to 5. She has received the symbolic name of *Hope.*

Mary was born on December 28, 1963. She narrated her story to me:

"I was raised in a Catholic milieu (environment). I attended Mass on Sundays but it was marginal, as a routine. My heart was not in it. In April of 1988, I made a pilgrimage to Medjugorje. I went to Confession to Fr. Pavich. I realized I had to change my life. Upon my return, I quit my position (traveling salesperson), where I was exposed to unfavorable influences, and I returned to my family who live in Wisconsin. There I read the messages of Medjugorje. I wanted to live them. I took the time to do this. I heard the voice of Jesus: *Would you leave your family for Me?*

"I did not understand then what He meant. I received other messages: *Write to Fr. Jack.*

At that time, at the beginning of August 1988, Gianna and Stefanie came separately to see Fr. Spaulding, talking about Mary Cook, whom neither really knew. They only followed their messages. She was one of the six already seen by Gianna in her vision.

Accordingly, Mary decided to leave Wisconsin and return to Scottsdale (Fr. Jack, whom she came to see, was amazed by the convergence of the messages).

"Was it a locution?" I asked her. "Did you hear a distinct voice telling you to return?"

"No, it was through the heart" (making a gesture suggesting from the interior).

She states that since then, Jesus talks to her nearly every day and she feels His presence throughout the day. She felt overwhelmed by this grace and dared not mention it at the prayer group on Friday evening. All this was too new for her. She also would say to herself at times, "Am I going crazy?"

But interior peace and warmth reassured her. It was fortunate for her, because her family fought against this apparently absurd change. Mary was closely bound to her family.

"It was hard," said she.

Her family, being concerned about helping her, wrote to her bishop asking him to intervene.

"She seemed to have fallen into a Satanic group; her communications appear like channeling," they reported.

In view of the wave of "religion without faith" which is developing these last years, many Christians and priests are justified in distrusting locutions. There are many false clairvoyances, among both Christians and others, and I have often heard of "channeling." We can allow that these troubled communications are coming less from subjectivity than from occult forces of the cosmos.

Mary found out about all these proceedings when going home to visit her family in July 1991, and better understood then the warning that she had received from Jesus. *Would you leave your family for Me?*

Before this period of grace which had started at the end of her stay in Wisconsin, Mary's life was troubled with anxiety. She had been tempted to slide into alcoholism. But this temptation ceased and she found peace. Previous worries are now replaced by compassion and mercy for others. She attends Mass daily. She is assiduous to the adoration of the Blessed Sacrament exposed in the Tabernacle building of the parish. She states she has had two apparitions of the Blessed Virgin. She also has trouble describing her.

"It is a presence more than an image. Jesus is also," she stated. "They are more interior visions than apparitions." She is overwhelmed by the beauty of Our Lady.

The past few years she managed a pre-school ("The Precious Ones Pre-School"). She now teaches young children ages 3 to 5, and enjoys this work a great deal. She has the gift of discernment.

She is a Eucharistic Minister in the parish like most of the others in the group.

Father Spaulding was her spiritual director, but she now has recourse to another priest and an 80 year old woman who has become a great companion to her. She has a need to confide and to receive help. Mary used to lean toward change and flight.

"But Our Blessed Mother has given me assurance and stability," she says today.

If she experiences occasional assaults from Satan, who tries to frighten her, she overcomes them in peace and in trust in Him who has brought her this new life.

4. Steve Nelson

Steve, 25 years old, was born the 6th of August, 1966—(the day of the Transfiguration). He is bursting with strength and health. He has a talent for singing and is successful in his business. He is in partnership with a friend in a business of repairing and painting houses. They are the sole owners and workers in this enterprise.

"Four years ago," (December 1987), he told me, "I met Susan Evans (the first of the six). I realized that my life was leaning more toward materialism and that I should develop my faith. Susan Evans, associated with the young adult prayer group, sought me out. She contacted my mother, who relayed this message: 'She wants to talk with you.' This message had no meaning for me. But Susan met me in front of the church one day and she was the catalyst of my good intentions."

Steve has kept a great esteem for and friendship with Susan:

"She is special! No one will ever know what she has suffered!"

He, bursting with health, joy and vitality, understands Susan's trials the most of all. He continues:

"Since September 16, 1988, I have been part of the young adult prayer group. On September 18, I saw Fr. Jack, who became my spiritual guide.

"Before, I used to go to Mass only on Sunday. Now, I go every day."

"You are able to manage this considering you have to work?"

"Yes, I attend the evening Mass at 5:30 p.m. I felt I needed to do something and I did not know what. I had not received any messages."

"And, have you had some since? When?"

"I knew in my heart that I had to do something for others (now I lay hands on people in prayer with the rest of the group). I have never received messages for other people. None of the messages printed in the books were received by me. I have received messages for myself for guidance in my personal life."

"For example?"

"I used to live 24 miles away, so it was difficult for me to attend church. I lived close to the rodeo stadium. I had a passion for the sport of roping. Everything was going well. I had started to become known and invited throughout America."

"What is this sport all about?"

"While you are riding on a horse, you try to lasso a calf and in record time, tie the hind legs together with one front leg. The person who accomplishes this the fastest wins."

"Have you won many times?"

"Yes."

"What? Trophies, medals?"

"No, belt buckles."

He has dozens of them at home...souvenirs of a frivolous time.

"Our Lady asked me to offer this up and give my heart totally. I had to choose between rodeo and God. I loved that sport. I reflected. This took about a week. Finally, I decided. I gave it up."

"How did your trainers and your supporters react?"

"They did not understand. The boss said: 'It is a mistake. You have potential, a future.' Sometimes all this comes back to me."

"After this decision, did anything new happen?"

"I became more aware of people and their problems. I had more compassion. A prayer life became more meaningful. I received the grace of discerning the presence of the evil one, who would follow behind me, and I received the grace of overcoming temptations."

It is no small matter to restrain or re-channel such a powerful and generous nature. He confesses regularly with humility and lucidity.

"You have received the grace to overcome temptation. What other graces have you received?"

"I have also received the graces to not forget morning prayer, to commit myself and to discern unfavorable places (night clubs and other such places) where the evil one attracts me."

"Do you fast?"

"On Wednesday and Friday."

"What kind of fast?"

"Bread and water and sometimes only one meal, depending on the work I have to do."

"How much (quantity) bread do you take?"

"About four slices per meal."

"Do you feel better the next day after fasting. Thursday and Saturday?"

"Yes, but I eagerly await eating in the morning!"

His robust and bountiful nature must give him a good appetite.

"Sometimes the tempter suggests to me: 'If you abandon the work you are doing for the Blessed Virgin, I'll give you anything.' "

"You hear a voice?"

"No, not a voice, but a clear communication, a tempting promise, nothing precise except that I would be able to obtain whatever I would want very easily."

Steve says he discerns the presence of the devil, when he is near him or within a group, somewhat like an antenna. He is warned and is not afraid. The devil has only to stand in front of this athlete as would the young bulls in his former rodeo days.

"Are you married?"

"No, I am single." (He will be married in June, 1992).

"Do you receive communications from Jesus and Mary?"

"From both of them."

"Frequently? Monthly? Weekly? Daily?"

"It is when I have a problem and need guidance."

"Would it be more of an inspiration or a light rather than a locution?"

"Yes, it is not a voice."

"When it is the devil, is it more of a voice?"

"Sometimes he tells me with great intensity: 'You will have a much better life if you abandon this work for the parish.' "

"When you lay hands on people, do they ask for advice?"

"I do not like publicity. I do not like to be the center of attention. This embarrasses me. I only answer what is asked of me."

"Do you have anything to add?"

"I went to Medjugorje in 1989. While I was praying in front of the cross on Mt. Krizevac, I felt the presence of the Blessed Virgin. She told me: *If people prayed more in front of the Blessed Sacrament, they would not need to come to Medjugorje. The only reason I appear here is to bring the children back to Jesus.* It was not a locution but a perception."

He has made but one pilgrimage to Medjugorje. He has received the symbolic name of *Faith*. Not only has he faith, but he has humility.

"I came to understand that there is only one difference between Peter and Judas. Both of them denied Jesus—the same weakness. But Peter recognized his offense and the mercy of God. Judas did not believe he could be forgiven. Similarly, if I sin but have confidence in God, I will be forgiven. I can sin again, although I refrain. . .Realizing that I am a sinner, I am more realistic in helping other people. I go forward like St. Peter walking on the waves toward Jesus."

Where is he going? He has made himself available to God alone.

"I believe with all my heart that there is a God and that He is a great God. I believe that if I really have faith in Him, He will guide me and take care of me."

Just as he has not ruled out marriage, he has thought also about priesthood, if Our Lord so wishes. He remains open to His will. He is now one of the leaders of the young adult prayer group.

He does not receive locutions or messages—only interior inspirations which are guiding his life. Our Lady guides his life entirely.

He has a distaste for publicity, although he is sure and firm enough to be sure of his identity when he is in the saddle.

"I am only an instrument. If people had more faith, they would not need me," he says.

5. Wendy Nelson

Wendy Nelson is Steve's sister. She is blond and friendly like him. The family comes from the plains of South Dakota, the wide open spaces of the western United States. Both of them have a western accent. They have a younger sister, Jenny, who is 16 years old. Their father works for a large oil company.

Wendy was the fifth one to contact Fr. Jack during the summer of 1988 following locutions received since spring of that year. He helped her to discern.

I met her soon after meeting her brother. She resembles him physically, although she is less robust and inward. She is perfectly wholesome and calm, and she reflects a profound spiritual depth. Wendy was born on the feast day of the Assumption, August 15, 1969.

"What did you do before 1989?" I asked her.

"I was a student at Arizona State University and I taught young children part-time. But I did not have any aim in life. I was not happy. My mother was praying for me. In the spring of 1988, she invited me to accompany her to the prayer group on Thursday night. At that time there were only 30 people. I enjoyed that experience. One day in the spring of the same year, I heard an interior voice saying: *Would you give up everything for Me?* I answered 'yes' at once. I did not know where I was going in life, but I had confidence in Jesus."

"How did you know it was Jesus?"

"In my heart."

"You were sure?"

"Yes!" (very emphatically). "I went to Confession to Fr. Jack. When I prayed, I would receive lessons from Jesus, locutions also, about twice a week at no specific time. Soon after, Fr. Jack assembled all the young people in his office. There were then six of us. This was at the end of the summer (probably the end of August). During this meeting we all shared our experiences. It was a real sharing. From then on I started to focus on the poor."

"Where are the poor in this rich and luxurious city?"

"In the south of the city, there is a suburb where illegal Mexican immigrants live. There are drug problems there."

"But how would they have money for drugs?"

"They sell them. And there is prostitution."

"In what way were you of help to them?"

"I lived with Mother Teresa's religious order for a year and a half."

"Did you ever see her?"

"Twice, once in Phoenix and another time in San Francisco, where she has other religious houses."

"Are you still associated with Mother Teresa?"

"No, right now I am studying sociology at the University, in order to learn to better serve the poor. I hope to return."

"Are you entertaining the thought of getting married some day?"

"Our Lord will guide me."

"What changes have taken place in your life?"

"When I was in college, I did not recite the Rosary; I would not go to Mass unless I felt like it, more or less once a month. I was not happy. I was searching."

"And now?"

"I attend Mass daily and the Thursday night prayer group.

When I worked with the nuns, helping them and sharing their life, I came to understand that it was also my calling."

"In regard to sociology, would that be of use to you, would it help you?"

"I think so. I understand more. A nun's life is very saintly. As of now I am involved in parish affairs."

"Do you plan entering Mother Teresa's community?"

"I will see."

"Have you had locutions or apparitions?"

"In 1990, in the autumn, I saw Our Blessed Mother for 3 to 5 minutes. It was on Thursday night during the prayer group. I was praying with my eyes closed and I had this locution: *Open your eyes and look at me as a child looks at her mother.* Then Our Lady came out of the statue. She was smiling. She did not talk. Then she went back into the statue. This had a great impact on my life."

"Does she look like the statue?"

"Much more beautiful!" (She said this with an expressive smile.) "She looks young, about 20 years old."

"Can you describe what she looks like?"

"She was dressed in blue, has blue eyes and brown hair which was visible under her veil."

"Her feet, were they touching the ground?"

"No, the distance was a couple of feet from the ground," (as she motioned with her hand to explain).

"On a cloud, like in Medjugorje?"

"No. . .I was looking at her face."

"Was it an interior vision?"

"No, she was near and she was very real." When she appeared, I had my eyes closed. She told me to open my eyes and I saw her."

The symbolic name for Wendy is *Strength*. This name would be more fitting for her brother, Steve, from his apparent strength. But she has interior strength, more tranquility (calm), a serene and graceful strength.

6. Jimmy Kupanoff

The sixth young person to join the spiritual sharing in early September 1988, was Jimmy Kupanoff, born on May 26, 1968. He is the eldest in a family of six children (three sisters and two brothers). He is the sixth of the initial group. Jimmy is studying Communications at the University of Arizona where he is a junior. He likes to write music. Religion made little sense to him before. He attended Mass on Sundays, but not regularly. His family was Catholic, but not fervent. Upon reading about Medjugorje in 1985, he made a pilgrimage there with his family and his girlfriend—a painful trip for him. He was having doubts about God. But two years later he was to experience the presence of God during a second pilgrimage (1987). This experience deepened on his return.

His entire family went through an intensive conversion and began living a prayerful life. When his family moved (transferred) to Ohio, he remained in Scottsdale and lived with his grandparents, who invited him to join St. Maria Goretti Parish.

"I knew that great things would be happening," he remembers.

He has a good relationship with Fr. Spaulding and had started to work with the teenagers in the parochial *Life Teen* program. He lived in the rectory for a period of time.

In the beginning of 1988, he met Mary Cook (the third in the group of six). They became very close. They shared many problems and decided to commit themselves to a more spiritual life. It was then that Mary decided to return to her family in Wisconsin. Also at this time, Jimmy's best friend died of cancer. He felt terribly abandoned.

Mary Cook returned to Scottsdale. She had changed noticeably and so had he. They diligently attended the Friday night prayer group. He received a special message through Gianna, and another from Estela Ruiz, a visionary from Phoenix. This message invited him to come up to be prayed over after the Thursday night service to consecrate his life to Our Lady. He was reluctant.

Father Spaulding informed him about the initial six young people, all called to see Our Blessed Mother one day.

"There are five already. . .you are the sixth," he told him, according to Gianna's premonitory vision.

Jimmy reflected and complied. He made his consecration and submitted. A long message from Stefanie was given to him. Our Blessed Mother was telling him how she had waited for him during his reservations.

Shortly after, his sister with whom he had had some differences, came to see him in tears, and they reconciled. Father Spaulding reiterates his being part of the group of six.

Jimmy has received personal locutions during his prayer time. During one of them, he saw himself in the future, in the form of a Knight. He felt it was symbolic, showing him the need for patience.

His life has changed. His relationships are more centered on the Bible. He is searching, perhaps for a vocation. Like the others, he was guided spiritually by Father Jack. Sensing Mary's call, he asked for counsel because something within him was resisting. He is conscious of the fact that he needs help.

Prior to his return to the university, he was active in the Thursday and Friday night prayer groups and has received locutions there.

"When Our Lady talks to me, it is not a voice, but my heart burns," he says. "When Our Lord talks to me it burns even more. The results are good inspirations and initiatives."

None of his locutions were published in the messages book. He does not have collective messages for the group. He receives personal advice only.

Since his conversion, he has made other pilgrimages to Medjugorje, the first in 1988—with profound experiences.

Our Lord and Our Lady have entered into his life. Still, he struggles to do what Our Lady asks of him. His spiritual growth, like the others', is on the right track. They recognize conversion as a daily process.

He has received the name of *Compassion*.

7. Stefanie Staab

Stefanie Staab, of whom we spoke before, did not become part of the group until the important meeting held at the end of summer 1988. The group of the original six was then expanded.

Our Lady had asked her to participate in the Friday night prayer group in September 1988. She has had messages for the group, but no apparitions. She also participates in the Monday night prayer group for the "teens" in the Tabernacle building. She has received locutions, which came as a surprise to her, first from Our Lady in 1988, and then from Our Lord in 1989. They continue.

8. James Pauley

James Pauley, born on the 17th of April 1971, is the youngest of the group. He is also the tallest—six feet three inches. On weekends he plays basketball.

He is a student at a community college in Scottsdale, one of the three universities in the area. He is calm, modest and sensitive. His faith is solid. He bears the symbolic name of *Courage*.

"About six years ago," he told me, "at the beginning of August 1985, I went on a retreat conducted by Fr. Spaulding. I experienced a profound presence of God—that He exists and that He loves me. From this point on, my life was different. I do not have visions or apparitions."

He went to Medjugorje in 1987 and there he was to acquire a new relationship with Our Lady.

In 1989, he became part of the group of young people which Gianna had seen in a previous vision. She thinks he will receive locutions or apparitions.

"Are you impatient?"

"I have been waiting for three years. During the first year, I was impatient, but I became patient. I wait. God's will be done. The most important thing is the Mass. I attend Mass about four times a week and I participate actively in all three prayer groups, Monday, Thursday and Friday."

In addition to time spent at Mass during the week and attending prayer meetings, he spends long hours in personal prayer.

His involvement in parish work consists of preparing teenagers for Confirmation, youth ministry and leading various prayer groups. For a long period of time, he was the leader of the teen prayer group on Monday nights, until he reached the age of 20, April 17, 1991.

During the summer of 1991 he made a fruitful retreat of five days in a Monastery in the desert in New Mexico.

He is dedicated to serving the poor. He participated in the building of a house for an indigent family and accompanied Wendy on a mission to Mexico in a similar service.

9. Annie Ross Fitch

Annie Ross, born in St. Louis, May 18, 1963, was the last one to meet with Fr. Spaulding one Thursday in April 1989. (In a premonitory vision Gianna had seen her, but from the back only.)

Having completed her college studies in Alabama and then Phoenix, she took a job in finance and real estate, then later opened her own flower shop. She has received the symbolic name of *Humility*.

She suffered a trial when her marriage to a Moslem on August 18, 1984, ended in an annulment. She had taken a job as a real estate agent to supplement the family income while he was finishing his studies, but the union did not last. When I interviewed her, she was preparing for marriage to someone more suited for her, and a Christian besides. Her fiance was with her. The marriage was planned for February 19, 1992.

Annie is an imposing, large-boned person. There is an openness about her which tends to her being rather talkative. Crowning her smiling face is an ample head of blond hair.

She grew up in a wealthy family. At the present time her existence is quite modest. The following is the essence of my interview with her:

Laurentin: What was your experience?

Annie: On March 31, 1989, during the Thursday night prayer group, I heard a voice: *Do you want to give me your heart? You must make the decision either for me or against. It is your decision to give it to me or not.* Soon I understood that it was the Blessed Virgin. It was a locution without a vision. When I returned home, she said to me: *My child, I wish for you to write.* I did not understand. I asked 'Excuse me?' She repeated without being precise. I had to write. I started to write without knowing where it would lead. I heard the harmonious voice of Our Lady and she was guiding my hand. I wrote three pages. I was filled with peace and joy. I told Fr. Jack what had happened. Our Lady started again two or three days later. I put the messages in an envelope for the pastor not knowing what else to do and not daring to see him. My handwriting is small and fine. But when my hand is guided thusly, my handwriting is larger and straighter. I continued to receive messages. Fr. Jack told me: 'Don't talk about it to anyone. Obey.' "

Stefanie Staab and Vassula Ryden (from Switzerland) have similar experiences.

"Starting June 10, 1989, Our Lord started to talk to me," continued Annie. "Sometimes I would be able to hear the messages, so I would write them in my own handwriting (much smaller than when my hand is guided). Before writing, I dialogue with Jesus and Mary."

Laurentin: What difference is there between the respective dialogues?

Annie: Mary has a soft voice. Our Lord has a strong voice. It took me some time to understand Jesus. I was very impressed with this voice, His tone: His powerful and divine presence. I was awestruck by His majesty. It was hard to understand why He was addressing Himself to me. I felt unworthy to receive this communication.

Laurentin: This taught you humility?

Annie: I hope so! (She smiled.) After this I started to see future events.

Laurentin: Concerning?

Annie: The parish and the world: Sometimes in dreams. On December 28, 1989, Our Blessed Mother appeared to me for the first time. It was on a Thursday. She did not talk. She had warned me.

Laurentin: How was she?

Annie: Like transparent, wearing a white mantle and veil and a gray dress.

Laurentin: Like in Medjugorje: gray-silver. Was she wearing a crown?

Annie: I do not remember. Sometimes she appears all in white. Sometimes she carries roses, symbolic of our prayers. *The roses are your prayers,* she says. She told me not to be afraid, to have confidence in God. She appears up from the ground. (Annie indicated with her hand.) Her feet are bare. When she appears, she comes out of the statue. First, there is a bright light and then it is as though the statue transforms itself into Our Lady. But she does not resemble the statue. She looks young—18 to 20 years old. Her eyes are a beautiful blue, her eye lashes are dark.

Laurentin: Does she appear far from you or near you?

Annie: About ten feet away. Sometimes she comes forward.

Laurentin: Have you touched her?

Annie: She kissed me once, it was warm. I experience an indescribable love when she touches me or kisses me. I am not intimidated by her anymore. I am very much at ease with her.

Laurentin: And Our Lord, have you see Him?

Annie: I do not see Him as a person in front of me but as a vision.

"Our Lady asked me if I wanted to see Heaven, Purgatory and Hell," Annie stated.

"Heaven and Purgatory, I answered, but not Hell, I would be afraid." She led me across a bridge (in spirit, not in body). I could hear lamentations, cries, without seeing the people. It was as though I were looking from a plane, in a fog, not seeing even silhouettes. These invisible persons were asking me for help."

Laurentin: And Heaven?

Annie: In Heaven, there was a large door (gate) without a frame, an opening. Jesus was in the opening. We walked on a sidewalk that seemed made of gold. There were plants, flowers, more beautiful than those on earth. We walked along the sidewalk. We came up to the throne of Jesus and Mary. They took their places. There was a place that seemed to be empty. It was the throne of God. He spoke but I could not see Him. His voice was even more powerful than that of Jesus. Jesus told Him: *I present this child in order that she would be purified.*

"The Father asked me why I was crying," Annie said, and she replied: " 'Because I am not worthy to be in Your presence,' and He told me that no one is worthy to be in His presence. He blessed me and we returned."

Laurentin: Did you see angels and the chosen ones (saints)?

Annie: No.

Laurentin: Then it was deserted?

Annie: No, it was very beautiful but I could only observe Jesus.

Sometime later (in a different church, in front of the Blessed Sacrament), Annie says Our Lady asked if she would like to return to Purgatory.

Annie: 'Yes,' I answered. I took the hand of Our Lady. She reassured me by telling me not to be afraid. I had been prepared to see Purgatory because she had asked me to pray for the souls who are being purified. I was on the same narrow bridge, and underneath this bridge, I saw the same thing. I heard a lot of voices and lamentations. 'Are there different levels?' I asked Our Lady. She said yes, and asked if I wanted to visit them.

"At the very bottom of Purgatory, I saw souls without their bodies surrounded by flames—being burned but not consumed. There was a wall and balls of fire were coming out of the wall. I asked her what it was and she told me that the fire was propelled from Hell but that it could not pierce through the wall. I asked to leave this level.

"We went to different levels. We stopped at the level where the most abandoned were—very sad. This level was somewhat more clear. I could see the pain—sorrow of these sad and abandoned persons. But as we neared the highest level, Heaven became visible, and angels reassure them—those who have made it up to this point have hope and are able to see the chosen ones being taken into Heaven. It was sad and happy at the same time because they are so near as to touch Heaven, without being able to enter. This was in October 1989."

I am perplexed with this vivid description of Purgatory by Annie because souls are invisible. I continued by asking:

Laurentin: This vision is important for you?

Annie: The important thing is that I have given her my heart and I am at her disposal. My mission consists in loving everyone. Mary told me that if I refuse to receive people (be accessible to people) she will stop appearing to me. She has asked me to talk about conversion of heart and of life, the Sacraments, to pray for priests, religious, seminarians, for the souls in Purgatory, and to suffer for the salvation of mankind.

Laurentin: What changes has all this brought into your life?

Annie: Before, I was a superficial Catholic. Now I go to Mass daily and I pray several hours a day. I do have difficulty in praying the Rosary but I manage to recite it at the prayer meeting on Thursday. Jesus explained why I was having difficulty and He invited me to change the way I say it. He told me to pray in my heart. At the beginning of the apparitions, Jesus had warned me that my prayer will be to offer my life. Our Lady has asked me to pray three times a day.

Annie always welcomes the visits of people after work. She is very busy but generous with her time.

On July 10, 1990, she said she received this prayer of consecration:

> Sacred Heart of Jesus, I consecrate to You my words, my body, my heart and my soul, in order that Your will be done through me this day.

On September 12, 1991, Annie said Our Lady warned her: *I will no longer appear to you regularly, only on your birthday and in time of need and necessity.* A trial period followed for Annie. It was the Spiritual Night and feeling of abandonment. She ceased writing in her journal until Christmas. But, she said that Our Lady appeared to her on December 27.

On February 15, 1991 she was officially informed that her marriaged had been annulled. It was then that she announced her engagement to a fine man who shares her faith.

During this period of time, the written messages that she claims to receive became more sporadic. Our Lady made known that she was going through a period of purification and preparation for her mission, Annie stated to me.

It was at this time that I met her, on July 31, 1991. We will later see the unfolding developments.

In defining this group of nine from Scottsdale, it would be well to mention two other persons who play a functional role: Carol Ameche and particularly the pastor, Fr. Jack Spaulding, whose key role is involved on all levels.

Carol Ameche

Carol Ameche, mother of a large family and a professional singer, has played a linking role, similar to that of a spiritual mother facilitating the contact among the nine. She has kept a chronology of the events and undertook the typing of the messages which was instrumental in their being published. She welcomes and meets with many visitors.

Fr. Jack Spaulding

Father Jack Spaulding, previously introduced above, holds the special key to this group. He had the insight to acknowledge and discern the charisms, however disconcerting they were, and assumed the responsibility, heavy and risky as it was. He brought the nine together and guided their progress. He is the spiritual director for some of them.

According to Carol Ameche, Father Jack supposedly was

to be the spiritual father and spiritual guide of the group, part of his mission, according to a message received by Gianna. But this instruction is not exact. The visionaries remain free to choose the priest they want to guide them. There are some among them who have chosen other spiritual directors, notably, Father Ernest Larkin, Carmelite and member of the investigating commission, Father Robert De Grandis or Father Robert Faricy, S.J.

Being pastor, Father Spaulding is the coordinator of the happenings, a particularly responsible and difficult task.

First of all, as pastor he finds himself uncomfortably situated on two levels, as many other pastors are. These levels should preferably be separate in order to avoid ambiguous interferences:

• Exteriorly: The organizing and administrative authority of which the law is transparent, definitive.

• Interiorly: The spiritual direction of conscience and confession of which the law is secrecy.

In a climate of spiritual paternity which demands an ensemble of rare conditions, the two could coincide. No doubt this is probably why certain visionaries, without lacking confidence in their pastor, preferred seeking spiritual help from other priests who are less over-burdened. In view of these facts, Father Jack himself has had to refuse other newcomers who present themselves to him. He is unable to attend to everyone's needs.

In fact, not only does he have to coordinate the visionaries (each one very different from the other) in a direct line toward the Holy Spirit, but he has to blend this group with the parish (we will come back to the difficulty of this task). He is responsible for overseeing the whole ensemble (overall picture) before the bishop and his commission and also other sensitive tasks.

Attending to all these functions is overwhelming. On all levels, he has to counterbalance considerable tensions, those which we observe in all living communities, since the Acts of the Apostles. The benevolence of Luke evidently blurred abundant conflicts; Paul the Apostle manifests them even more when he alludes to his differences publicly with Peter; and what of the unpleasant conflicts that Paul had to resolve in the community of the Corinthians (*I and II Cor.*), or John in the Epistle addressed to his communities (*2 John* 7-11; *3 John* 9-10).

Father Spaulding, whom many can attest to regarding his exceptional personality, was able to guide with comprehension and authority (not without difficulty) this assortment of problems and anxieties. It could happen that he could be momentarily tense, or to experience difficulty in bringing about order and mercy. And certainly these unilateral practices could lead to disorder and to an increase of conflicts without God's grace.

All things considered, we can but admire the mastery (assisted by the Holy Spirit) with which Father Jack assumes his duties and in giving first priority to prayer. His talents as an organizer and his continuous presence make for a good example, a key task in the life of the Church.

Pastoring a parish is a task that the Council of Trent had valorized, and that the Council of Vatican II undoubtedly devalued too much in its concern to rearrange the episcopal duty. Many bishops had difficulty supporting the permanent authority that the Council of Trent had given to the pastors.

What is odd in the position of Father Spaulding is that not only is he the advised and respected authority, but he is also part of the special group. He considers himself as the tenth one.

In fact, after some preliminaries which we will come back to in the following chapter, he became, much to his surprise, the echo of Jesus through his own homily, starting on the 23rd of February, 1989.

Chapter 5

Spiritual and Charismatic Development

It is important to reassess the spiritual and charismatic development of Scottsdale from the standpoint of Fr. Jack Spaulding (the responsible coordinator of the events), the spiritual growth of the visionaries, the formation of the prayer groups, the expansion of the fruits, and the particular curriculum of each of the nine. This review is necessary in order to clarify the genesis of the phenomena.

Birth of the First Two Prayer Groups— November/December 1987

Most of the visionaries knew their pastor and had received intermittent counseling from him. Susan Evans' visit to him in the spring of 1987 made him aware of the first charismatic awakening. But it was primarily his first two pilgrimages to Medjugorje (in June for his television program; then, with his parishioners in October 1987), that lit the spark. Thus were born the first prayer groups:

- The teenagers, 13 to 19 years of age, in November,
- And an adult group, the 3rd of December.

The prayer groups consisted of traditional prayers, not charismatic. The Rosary was recited and Mass was celebrated similar to the liturgical model of Medjugorje, without any aforethought of the extraordinary future events. These prayer groups blended harmoniously with the life and tradition of the parish which is centered on the Eucharist.

48

First Message—June 1988

The awakening of the charisms did not occur at the end of the third pilgrimage to Medjugorje (March 1988) but after the fourth visit in June, when Gianna met Wayne Weible and Vicka. Shortly after her return she started to receive private messages, and shared this event with Fr. Jack.

"I made the discernment according to the criteria of the Church," said Fr. Spaulding: "Good relationship with family and other people, sense of duty, conformity of messages with faith and Scripture. Is the person attentive to the Sacraments, especially reconciliation? A week later (near the end of June 1988) Stefanie came to me.

"Stefanie is a brilliant individual. She had started coming to the prayer group, then one day she told me, 'I hear a voice.' She received long messages, theological teachings in essence.

"A week later, Steve Nelson came to me. Same thing; a woman's voice was telling him: *Come to my Son and pray.*

"Eight months later (start of 1989) he gave up his favorite sport, roping. Two others came. Same story. None of them really knew one another. They were fundamentally yuppies—young people more interested in the materialistic world."

After her return from Medjugorje (June 1988), Gianna started to receive personal messages.

"In July 1988, after the prayer group," relates Fr. Spaulding, "Gianna tells me: 'I think I have received a message for the parish.' I told her to write it down and to bring it to me. This was the beginning of the messages from Our Lady for the prayer group. And so, Gianna wrote it and brought it to me and the following week I read it at the Thursday night service.

"This small sign seemed to be an approval of the faithfulness of the prayers of the parish. It was in a way confirming the importance of the communication of God in our hearts."

The first published message Gianna received from Our Lady, dated July 14, 1988, has been quoted in the *"I Am Your Jesus of Mercy"* book.

My children, open your hearts to Jesus... (Vol.
I, page 109).

Gianna says that in August she received the first message
from Jesus, during the Thursday evening prayer group
meeting:

> *I am in you and you are in Me. We are one. My
> Spirit is in you and My Spirit gives you strength,
> wisdom and love. You live in the house of the
> Lord.''*

The second message, which begins the published lessons,
was:

> *My child, I would like you to start being and liv-
> ing the holiness of Me.* (Vol. I, page 9).

Formation of the Group of Six
(July-September 1988)

On this day, July 14, 1988, Gianna claimed a vision of
the group of six and less clearly, the other three, as the group
was being formed.

In the same month of July, Gianna says she started to
receive not only private messages, but messages for the parish, those that are published today. She shared them with Fr.
Spaulding who remained perplexed. Henceforth, she
presented messages which were to become a regular part of
the Thursday meeting. Fr. Spaulding would read them the following Thursday (Vol. I, pages 109-119). Starting September
20, messages from Our Lord were apparently added.

Assumption in Medjugorje

In the month of August, 1988, Father Jack returned to
Yugoslavia the fifth time to celebrate the closing of the
Marian Year.

> "Our Lady talked to me twice. They were locu-
> tions in the heart, but so clear that I looked around

to see who was speaking. It was on the feast day of August 15th. She told me: *You have to walk by faith and not by sight.*

"I did not know where all this would lead me. On August 15th, I was celebrating Mass in St. James Church, and after communion, I was complaining to Our Blessed Mother about the commercialism in Medjugorje of which I was thoroughly disgusted. I questioned if she was still there. A voice said to me: *I am here, and I am going home with you.*

"Upon my return, other young people came to see me for the same reason. They were hearing voices. On December 6, 1988, the young adults formed a prayer group for themselves on Friday. When they began, there were 17; now there are 50 to 70 who attend.

"It was more an initiative from these people rather than a message or locution. Their ages range from 18 to 35. The format was of traditional prayer lasting one hour and a half, consisting of the Rosary, Chaplet of Divine Mercy and spontaneous prayer and the Mass."

In September 1988, Father Spaulding assembled the group of six previously and prophetically seen by Gianna. They exchanged their experiences, perfectly convergent, with their pastor who insisted on discretion and prudence.

Collecting and Publishing the Messages

"In September of 1988," confirms Fr. Spaulding, "Gianna told me that Jesus was giving her lessons. I thought: 'Now what?' She showed me her notebook and said: 'Our Lord wants these messages published.' I said: 'Let's wait.' She continued to prod me.

"She then asked Carol Ameche to collect and type these messages. Carol is a middle-age mother of a family, who has helped and supported the events at all levels—a help to the visionaries. She welcomes them; she is an organizer, and a confidant."

Two months later, in the fall, Our Lady is said to have advised Gianna that she wished to talk more directly to the

Thursday evening group. . .and not delay reading the message a week later by Fr. Jack. Now we will see Our Lady's wishes take an unexpected turn. Fr. Jack himself had a surprising and uncomfortable experience.

"In November 1988," he relates, "I found my mind completely blank before the homily at Mass. I could not even remember what the Gospel was. I had no remembrance of it. In this sudden confusion, I heard myself talking. It was not me who was talking, and I do not remember what I said. This left me completely drained. Gianna reported to me after Mass what Our Lady had told her:

> *I do not want that my children would have to wait a week to receive the message.*

" 'If you say yes, Our Lady will use you in this way now and then,' Gianna concluded."

From then on the message would often come through Fr. Jack's homily.

"In December 1988, I had the impression that it was Jesus, Who was talking through me because this time it was stronger. It seemed as though He was using me as a microphone. I cannot hear the words, they just come out. It is not me, nor my style."

The first such message that was published is dated February 23, 1989. It is as follows.

> *Children, I have risen from the dead. The Gospel has been fulfilled, and yet there are so many who do not believe.*
>
> *It is true. . .even when My Father raised Me to life, people did not believe, and they still do not. My dear ones, you do believe. I invite you, I beg you, to show your belief in your actions.*
>
> *Be grateful and hope-filled, so that the ones who are lost will come back. Show My Resurrection in your very selves, My dear ones. I love you, and I thank you for living My Resurrection. Maybe they*

will listen to you, and be saved! (Message Vol. I, page 131).

"During Lent 1989 no messages were received," specified Fr. Spaulding. "One time I tried to bring them about by myself but I could not."

It is not like we discover a recipe and we exploit it, but rather, it is the gratuitousness of God Who guides us through unexpected ways. It is thus at Scottsdale.

Estela Ruiz' Apparitions

Carol Ameche states that it was at that time, February 1989, that the group of nine learned about the apparitions of Estela Ruiz in south Phoenix, which also had started in December 1988, in another parish. Her husband had advised Fr. Jack of the apparitions and invited him to come to their home for discernment. In the process Estela advised Fr. Jack that special things were about to happen at St. Maria Goretti Parish involving Our Lady, unaware that they had already started.

In August of 1989, Fr. Jack, trying to discern Gianna's strong request to have the messages and lessons printed, sought the advise of several friends on the logistics of such an undertaking. It seemed very remote.

"A couple of days later," relates Fr. Jack, "I suddenly received a letter from The Riehle Foundation who had heard about the events in our parish and offered any assistance required. I was shocked and delighted. I called Bill and Fran Reck and they agreed to discern through prayer the possibility of taking on this responsibility." Three months later the first book, *"I Am Your Jesus of Mercy"* was released. It was right around this same time that Bishop O'Brien formed the investigating commission.

Emergence of the Charisms

Gianna had revealed to Fr. Spaulding a message of the Blessed Virgin that she would appear to her, then eventually to the others. Fr. Spaulding commented on this as originally being a concern.

"Nothing occurred. This caused me to doubt in my mind, but I came to understand that it would not happen immediately but later on."

On December 28, 1989, Our Lady alledgedly appeared to Gianna in the church, during the prayer meeting on Thursday evenings. She heard:

> *Why are you so surprised? Did I not tell you that*
> *I would appear to you first.*

Annie Ross claimed apparitions the following week at the same time as Gianna. At the time of my visit to Scottsdale, four visionaries reported apparitions of Our Lady: Gianna, Annie, Wendy and Mary. Those of Annie had ceased in October 1990, but with a promise that she would appear to Annie in times of need.

The visionaries state that there is a bright light which precedes the apparition of Our Lady, who comes out of the statue near the altar in the church. She is dressed in white. At times she carries roses. She comes as **Our Lady of Joy**.

Our Lady wants to be known also as **Our Lady of the Americas**, to fight against sin on Satan's home ground. "What we yuppies of Scottsdale can do, all the world can also. These young people were no more saints than others. Their spiritual growth is indicative of the fruits," says Fr. Spaulding.

The ten are convinced that the messages and the visions are less important than their conversions. Each one of them was asked to pray for the souls in Purgatory and also to fast.

The prayer meetings at St. Maria Goretti Parish include the celebration of the Mass as in Medjugorje. The group is invited to answer questions, but not expressly to go out and evangelize.

At the end of the prayer meeting, the visionaries present would gather in front of the altar with Fr. Spaulding to pray and lay hands on the people who needed prayers, spiritual or physical healing inordinately. But the line of people became longer and longer. In September 1991, Father Spaulding stopped this ritual because it was taking on too much importance, as well as too much time. He has replaced it with a global prayer at the end of the Mass, for all intentions presented.

A Climate of Discretion

Father Jack did not seek nor has he provoked these spiritual phenomena. They came spontaneously. He was the first one to be surprised. He welcomed the individuals in their extreme diversity. He was also overtaken by the same grace, in a different way.

He has gauged the importance of discernment as well as prudence, because these unusual phenomena can provoke reactions or oppositions in the parish where they occur. In Scottsdale, many are unaware, even some who attend the prayer group meetings. They have not noticed the particular charisms that the visionaries have. Even when the first book *"I Am Your Jesus Of Mercy"* was published, still the parishioners were not aware because the book was not being sold or promoted in the parish. Learning about it from strangers, they asked their pastor quite astonishingly:

"Why have you not told us? Is it true?"

As far as the bishop is concerned, Fr. Spaulding practices unconditional obedience. He has been asked to avoid all publicity and propaganda. This presented some conscious problems when The Riehle Foundation undertook the publication of the messages—they were not forbidden by any higher authority. But Fr. Spaulding was worried that it was not in conformity with the instruction of discretion given by the bishop. But Bill Reck answered: "I will take full responsibility. I release you of yours. The book is already being printed."

The first volume was released December 2, 1989, the second August 12, 1990, and the third in September 1991.

As many people came from long distances by bus to participate in the prayer groups, they parked in the parish's vast
parking area, but soon the bishop asked that this sign of
influx be avoided. In turn, Fr. Jack requested them to park
in the street, which happily in Phoenix can be accomplished
easily, because of the wide streets.

Discretion was observed on all spiritual levels.

Should We Hide the Light?

The discretion that Fr. Spaulding cultivates, spontaneously
and by obedience, is befitting to the accomplishment of the
spiritual works brought about by God's intimate gift. The
Holy Spirit works in ways strange to publicity. This discretion
is becoming more and more difficult: *"A city set on a hill
cannot be hidden."* said Jesus. (*Matt.* 5:14). And in this similar instance, it is better to have balanced information than
a confused dissimulation.

This is one of the problems of this book. In the course
of my interviews with the visionaries, I did not fail to observe
certain silences. The visionaries remain silent, secretive, or
discreet concerning certain graces private in nature, including
gifts of healing which are exercised unobtrusively.

And so this book remains divided between two exigencies:
discretion and manifestation of the truth.

CHAPTER 6

Bishop's Investigation

According to the criteria published by Rome in 1978, Thomas Joseph O'Brien, Bishop of Phoenix, wasted no time in leaning on these unusual phenomena. First of all he spoke personally with Fr. Jack Spaulding, his ex-Chancellor.

Nomination of the Commission

A year after the start of the events, in the summer of 1989, he nominated an investigating commission comprised of three members.

1. Father Ernest Larkin, Carmalite Discalced, theologian, mystic specialist (along the line of St. John of the Cross, who was strict concerning apparitions. Nevertheless, he had some, and Therese of Avila even more).
2. Sister Theresa Sedlock, OSF, noted for her competence in spirituality.
3. Dr. James Lange, psychologist, Ph.D.

The three commissioners did not make an exhaustive study, but an initial discernment starting with an overall examination to see if this religious phenomena and cult would have to be repressed or helped, according to the criteria established in 1978 by *The Congregation of Faith*. And so, they met with the pastor and taped the interview, but the tape was lost.

Then they interviewed the visionaries and locutionists in a group, not individually.

Two months later, at the end of October 1989, the Commission had established its report: rapidly, as was agreed. It was handed to the bishop. After reflection and prayer, Bishop Thomas J. O'Brien, Bishop of Phoenix, drafted his judgment.

The Judgment

This judgment was relayed to interested parties with mention of confidentiality—not for publication (Jan. 5, 1990).

But on January 18, 1990, the diocesan newspaper, *The Catholic Sun,* published it in full. After a certain period of time, the band of secrecy was lifted. The judgment became public domain. Here is the content:

> "When it came to my attention that certain individuals, including the pastor of St. Maria Goretti Church, Father Jack Spaulding, believed they were receiving teaching messages, in the form of locutions, from our Lord Jesus Christ and the Blessed Virgin Mary, I met with Father Spaulding to discuss these messages with him. Father Spaulding had an opportunity to explain the events as he believed they were occurring. Based on my conversation with Father Spaulding and other reports which I had received, I informed Father Spaulding that I would be appointing a Commission of Inquiry to investigate the events.
>
> "In situations such as this, where individuals believe they are having direct, extraordinary or miraculous interaction with God, the Blessed Virgin Mary, the angels or saints, it is the ordinary custom of the Church to investigate the matter in a calm, deliberate and prudent manner.
>
> "In my concern for the people involved and the welfare of the Church, I appointed, on June 25, 1989, a three-member Commission to inquire into the nature of these events. The members of this Commission were Father Ernest Larkin, O. Carm., Sister Therese Sedlock, OSF, and Dr. James Lange, Ph.D. These members were chosen because

of their expertise in the areas of theology, spirituality and psychology.

"At the end of October 1989 the Commission reported to me their conclusions and recommendations concerning the events at St. Maria Goretti Parish.

"The Commission concluded that the messages (locutions) 'are explainable within the range of ordinary human experience' and they continue by stating 'obviously we cannot know for certain whether or not the locutions or visions are miraculous in the true sense of the word. By miraculous we mean a mode of action beyond the ordinary laws of nature and caused by an exceptional, direct divine intervention.' In their opinion, the Commission members indicated: 'Because the events seem to us to be explained as human experiences and by ordinary human dynamics, we are constrained to conclude that they are within the order of nature and are not miraculous.' The Commission further stated, 'the commitment to the Lord and depth of faith in all the individuals involved are beyond question.' The Commission also said, 'Father Spaulding has demonstrated himself to be a good priest and he should be commended for his devotion to Our Lady.'

"After much prayerful discernment, I have accepted the conclusion drawn by the Commission and I have personally communicated this decision to Father Spaulding.

"I have approved the following recommendations of the Commission concerning the events at St. Maria Goretti Parish in Scottsdale, Arizona:

1. "The prayer meetings and public devotions at St. Maria Goretti may continue for the spiritual welfare of all concerned. There may not be, however, any *unequivocal* claim of miraculous

intervention. This is due to the absence of any external evidence that the messages are directly from Our Lord Jesus Christ or the Blessed Virgin Mary.

2. "In order to maintain the unity of the prayer group at St. Maria Goretti with the whole Church, I am establishing a 'Community of Discernment.' The Community of Discernment will: aid the prayer group in interpreting any future events; direct the development of devotion to Our Lady; monitor the circulation of any publications produced by the prayer group.

"I would like to restate the teaching of the Church that devotion to Mary springs from her position in Sacred Scripture where she accepts the role of Mother of the Savior, raises the child Jesus, and stands with Him at the cross. The reverence for her is summed up in the words of the angel Gabriel, *Rejoice, O highly favored daughter! The Lord is with you. Blessed are you among women* (*Luke* 1:28).

"Rooted in the faith of Catholics, the role of Mary is part of the mystery of faith. This role belongs to public revelation and to the deposit of faith handed over to the Apostles and presented by their successors in the official ministry of the Church. Private revelations and apparitions of the Blessed Virgin Mary in history have added greatly to the devotion of the people of God to their Church, have sustained countless nations during times of persecutions, and are a part of the rich devotional heritage of the Catholic people. However, even authentic devotions do not add anything new to our faith, but only recall what we have always believed. They remind us of our failure to practice our faith as we should; they call us to repentance and to a deeper and fuller faith in Jesus

Christ. In all times the Blessed Virgin Mary calls us to her son Who is Lord of all the ages.

"I would like to thank the members of the Commission of Inquiry for their diligent and prayerful work on this serious matter. In addition, I would like to commend Fr. Spaulding and the members of his prayer group for their spirit of prayerful cooperation. All of the parties in this matter have been motivated by a spirit of love for Our Lord, His Blessed Mother and our Church."

Briefly, the bishop recalls the classical doctrine: Devotion to the Blessed Virgin is founded on Scripture. (Objectively, apparitions would not add anything). There is nothing to admonish in the healthy and spiritual quality of the prayer movement in Scottsdale. It deserves only praise.

In the proper sense of the word, the Commission has not found proof of any miracles. That is to say, an extraordinary action from God transcending nature's laws. The Commission does not deny that there could be intervention from God or to the fact that there exists exceptional or extraordinary intervention. They only state that they do not have any proof. They believe that these phenomena could be explained in the framework of ordinary psychology. Therefore, these conclusions are prudent and reasonable. They uphold the rapidity of the investigation.

Evaluation

The commission leaves the question open and we can only regret that classical theology of these past centuries has narrowed the definition of supernatural as **extraordinary** and **inexplicable** in regard to the laws of nature. A more precise definition of supernatural and divine intervention aspects invite us to consider the following.

The visible and temporary signs of the power of God (miracles) could be, more or less unexplained or totally extraordinary, indeed inexplicable, by natural laws or even contrary to these laws.

As far as "miracles" are concerned, even the vocabulary of the Bible invites us to distinguish three aspects:

—On the side of **marvellous**—astonishing, from whence comes the word miracle (from latin *mirari*: to be astonished, and secondly: *admire*);

—The **prodigy—wonder** *(teraton)* more or less extraordinary or inexplicable; and

—The **sign**—more or less obvious from God's action (Greek: *Semeion)*.

These three components of miracles can be found in proportions and combinations at various degrees:

• More or less surprising—astonishing, obvious, admirable;

• More or less inaccessible to human reason; and

• More or less revealing of God's power.

The most important, in respect to the Bible, is not some prodigious way (which assumes more or less sorcery) or sensational (astonishing), but that which raises and transfigures man by faith, hope and love. This communication of divine life is not foreign to natural laws nor contrary to these laws, and yet, one day we will discover that this discreet action of grace was the greatest and the most beautiful prodigy that God has accomplished on this earth—misunderstood because of its being invisible. Grace cannot be perceived by human eye except by the real believers, even if this wonder escapes the established physical realm and the calculations of mathematics. Grace is invisible like God Himself. He thereby communicates His own nature and His own love to us. Hence, signs and wonders.

Moreover, God's profound action no longer has the character of "gratifying signs," which mark the spiritual life's first steps. The Dark Night and the crucifying trials of agony and abandonment are rather contrary signs. Even the psalmists complained of this to Our Lord. But Christ Himself underwent these trials. All this is not taken into consideration when discerning spiritual events.

We will come back to these theological facts, which are useful in clarifying the Commission's tentative conclusions. We will ask ourselves then, in what way is Scottsdale an eloquent sign of God's marvellous grace: for example in what measure do the healings which take place in this parish create a presumption that there could be miracles? (ch. 9).

At this time, let us hear what the members of the Commission had to say. Father Larkin states in the diocesan journal, *The Catholic Sun:*

> "No one was disturbed by the events, and other parish activities were not neglected. Certain people, however, remained indifferent. For example: One man who was interrogated about his opinion, rolled his eyes meaning to say that this was not for him."

Sister Theresa Sedlock expresses a regret:

> "I felt that they lacked a necessary openness for discernment. They were very sure to prove or defend that there were actual messages from Our Lord and from Mary addressed to them."

It is quite normal that a discerning member, commissioned because of a critical mind, (in accordance with today's faculty and also commissioned notably because of her competence in psychology) would be astonished by the *assurance* of the visionaries and would adopt a more relative point of view. But it is equally normal that the visionaries, who are enlightened by God by a personal contact with Him, would witness to the evidence received with the assurance as seen in the *Acts of the Apostles:* "Christian certitude" *(parrhesia)*. Mystical Theology, and even the Councils, admit that God can give to man certitudes, personal absolutes, although they would be unable to furnish proof.

In addition, according to Rahner and Congar, responding

to definitions too juridical in the belief of miracles and apparitions, that would be **"human faith"**. The visionaries can
receive from God evidence such as that derived from their
beliefs in **"divine faith."** This certitude is part of their
charism. This certitude is classical; it gives strength to their
testimony. Consequently, it could not be removed from them
as in the case of Bernadette, or more severely in Jeanne
Lebosse's case (from Pontmain).

But, however strong their interior evidence received by
grace, the visionaries are unable to demonstrate this evidence
"exteriorly" to reiterate the Commission's terminology. And
this interior character of their certitude (if they have certitude), nevertheless does not exempt them from obedience to
the bishop in what concerns the exterior order.

On the part of James Lange, psychologist, he states:

> "There is no aberration from a psychological
> standpoint in regard to Fr. Spaulding and the other
> persons who were examined. There are no indica-
> tions of deception or fraud. These people have
> Faith."

As far as the bishop is concerned, according to the same
article, he has attested that such events are part of the rich
spiritual heritage of a Catholic people. However, they do not
add anything new to our Faith but they "remind" us of our
everlasting Faith.

Acceptance by the Parish

Fr. Spaulding, the visionaries and the parish have accepted
this judgment in all respect, comprehension and obedience.
Their spiritual enlightenment was not shaken. They were confirmed in humility, modesty and discretion, which are part
of their experience.

CHAPTER 7

My First Visit to Scottsdale

I now have to relate the observations made during my trip there from Wednesday, July 31, to Friday, August 2, 1991. I spent much time with eight of the ten members of the group at St. Maria Goretti. In cases such as these, the occasion to meet and the direct contact are of great importance. Being an historian, I particularly appreciate this, having been limited to printed matter, archives research, and having to use imagination on certain written subjects. I have never seen Saint Bernadette! Direct observation of the facts is irreplaceable as far as spiritual discernment is concerned, much as is a clinical examination of the patient by the doctor.

Irreplaceable Contact

There is a quantity of things that written material cannot convey, notably, each visionary's own character: simplicity, naturalness, sincerity (or the contrary), and also each one's peculiarities as seen through the multiple traits which are evident beyond conversation. It was good to observe these young people not only in their diversity and differences, but also the harmony among them—their involvement into Phoenix's hub, a successful city created in a torrid but green oasis. The parish blends well with this harmonious and ardent city.

The parish is a bee-hive. Many live here. Many come and visit here and are welcomed. The church and the Tabernacle building are never deserted. The impeccable cleanliness is visible. Air-conditioning is provided in all buildings—a 100 degree Fahreinheit témperature making it more of a necessity than a luxury. One meets persons who have been healed, while the parish maintains complete discretion on these healings. Their point of view does not indicate an attitude of indifference.

The Mass

After the first interview, I concelebrated the evening Mass. The church was almost filled and many attend the daily morning Masses. The church was silent and prayerful. There was an impressive crucifix, a replica of a Salvador Dali painting, suspended above the altar—a downward view which focuses on the crown of thorns of Jesus Christ overlooking the people. This cross appeared detached from the stained-glass window, a scene of the Resurrection. Two statues framed the altar: To the right was Jesus of Mercy and to the left was Our Lady.

I attended the usual Thursday evening prayer meeting at 7:00 p.m. More than 500 persons were present. I had anticipated a Charismatic meeting but instead I found a classical, austere and traditional one, where the Rosary and Divine Mercy Chaplet are recited without commentary, slowly, in a contemplative rhythm. Each decade lasted about five minutes which was conducive to praying with your heart. Then there was Mass, including a homily, followed by praying for the sick and those who ask for prayers.

The pastor preached unaffectedly. The tone was discreet and neutral considering the fact that he is a television personality. No affectations were observed at church.

During the Rosary, they had me sit between Gianna and Annie. Annie was on my right and Gianna on my left. I was alerted that Our Lady might appear during the third decade. Many are unaware because their ecstasies are discreet.

"Will there be an ecstasy?" I had asked.

"We do not know," they told me.

The parish was unconcerned about scientific controls and experiments because they wanted to avoid any form of testing that would disturb prayer. There has not been any medical study. Uppermost in their minds were spiritual quality and maximum discretion.

I was about to forget this "happening" because of the monotonous but fervent recitation of the Rosary, but on the third decade of the Joyous Mystery Annie and Gianna knelt suddenly. Without wincing, a smile lit up their faces. The simple smile reflected an acknowledgment of seeing a loved one. The joyful contemplation was also a dialoguing one. Annie is more glowing in comparison to Gianna, who experiences many trials. Thus, the reaction was more interior. How different they are!

—Gianna, short, slender, brunette, intellectual and a technician, but sensitive ("a sweet kid. . .a nice person, she loves God," said Fr. Spaulding during his conference in St. Louis, Mo. on April 25, 1990). Her face reflects great interior substance under all that curly hair.

—Annie, blonde, tall and strong—her round face constantly expresses a great tenderness and a perfect openness.

Our Lady was apparently there for them. The dialogue was alive and natural, similar to Mejugorje. I regret to have to use these limited means to attempt these observations which had not previously been made. But this allowed comparison since I have been able to make my observations in other respects, according to what they have in common as well as their diversities.

These appeared to be totally similar to the ecstasies in Medjugorje and those of Rossana in Italy:

—Kneeling down quickly at the beginning of the ecstasy;
—Locution without sound (the voice disappearing at the start of the ecstasy); and
—The eyes fixed ardently and simply toward the invisible which they see.

Their gazes were fixed; undoubtedly an electro-oculagram would manifest the immobility of the pupils as was observed in Medjugorje. Before the ecstasy, the eyes were animated and blinking rapidly in order to observe the exterior world. At the beginning of the ecstasy, this active observation of the material world ceased, the eyes became fixed for a contemplation of a different nature, which was nonetheless intense and expressive.

Annie's eyelids did not blink, as those of Vicka in Medjugorje; Gianna's blinked a little less than normal, like Marija and Ivan in Medjugorje. Observation was confirmed by Dr. Mansour of Los Angeles, who observed an ecstasy of eight minutes, January 16, 1992.

All this indicates that there is indeed an ecstasy, that is to say, a disconnection with the ordinary world. The cessation of the changing perceptions of the natural environment conditions the perceptions of another world. It is an ecstasy without tension, twisting or catalepsy. The visionaries remain very natural, in attitude as well as in expression. The disconnection is not as profound as in Kibeho, but it is not the degree of disconnection that measures the quality of an ecstasy or of a communication. Rather, it appears that the less accentuated ones respond to a contact more simple, more natural, and evidently more removed from pathological components. Here there aren't any: it's beautiful, it's transparent.

I would presume to say that an encephalogram would manifest an alpha rhythm quite pure: that of a profound contemplation.

At Scottsdale, like in Medjugorje, the return to reality is accomplished smoothly: no falling, no fainting and no "resting in the spirit," unlike the case in Kibeho where the ecstasies are more profound and painstaking. The contemplation here is pure and clear. The supernatural does not alter nature.

The end of the ecstasy was without regret, without frustration, like the ending of a wonderful meeting and the return to customary activities. Like in Medjugorje, each visionary lowered her head spontaneously, each according to her character. Each one recollected herself happily. Our Lady had apparently disappeared from view but remained present. They did not see her any more but they had not lost her. They appeared to feel strong and capable enough to continue their painstaking existence filled with trials.

"What do you experience?" I asked.

"First of all, there comes a bright light behind the statue, and Our Lady appears in that light (another similarity with Medjugorje)."

At the end, Our Lady is said to disappear by rising, and a luminous cross manifests itself for a short time afterward, not unlike Medjugorje.

After Mass, Fr. Spaulding, along with the nine visionaries (or at least most of them who are present) met with those seeking prayer. The line was long, calm and collected.

I suggested that a medical examination would be beneficial from a physical standpoint concerning these phenomena: for the sake of coherence on the part of the receiver. But it was refused deliberately so that the technical preoccupation would not disturb the essential. This reminds me of Dr. Mangiapan's advice, then president of the *Medical Bureau of Lourdes*. He was besieged with the heavy responsibilities of affidavits at his talk with a group of Americans from the "Charismatic Renewal," concerning claimed healings:

"Do not go into the workings and dispersion of affidavits; stay with the natural character of the happening," he advised.

Visit to the Bishop's Office

Before leaving, on the 2nd of August, I went to the Bishop's office in Phoenix. I had written to the Bishop, advising him of my private trip. He sent me a friendly reply inviting me to meet with him. But he was absent at the time I went. I met with the Chancellor and I made known to him my impressions: how I situate Scottsdale among the multiple apparitions of today. It will be the subject of the following chapters.

CHAPTER 8

Discernment and Judgment

The event of Scottsdale is not a simple prolonging of the dynamics of Medjugorje. The trip to Yugoslavia was a stimulus, a catalyst, a source of conversion and of light for many parishioners. It awakened charisms. But it was not the only source of the spiritual movement in Scottsdale. Susan, the first one who met with Fr. Jack, had not gone to Medjugorje and Stefanie has never been there. The religious happening in Saint Maria Goretti Parish is not a mimicry, but the fruition of a grace coming from deep within, which has taken form interiorly like all life develops and flourishes under the auspices and inspiration of the Holy Spirit. The American background is in no way altered. The autonomy and the specificity are remarkable.

1. Diversity in Unity

The visionaries are very different in grace and in personality. What they have in common is age (from 18 to 32 at the start). Some were "fallen-away" Catholics after having been raised in a Catholic family. Each experienced some separation from church in various degrees of lukewarmness. There were never relationships with one another. Their cultural levels, their employment, their tastes and their preoccupations are ever so diversified—laborer and intellectual, outgoing and contemplative, men and women, etc.

Their respective graces are very diversified and they are aware of it. Some claim locutions only. Some claim visions or apparitions (I would like to point out the variation "nuance" between those two words, the second one indicating a more objective type of perception). From there the charisms are even more diversified. Unfortunately, the discretion of the visionaries and the pastor, stimulated by obedience, does not permit them to be open about their particular charisms. Our summary (Chapter 5) is not exhaustive.

When we inquire a little more, we notice that they have received important and coherent gifts in order to attend to the needs of the people in regard to giving counsel, charitable acts, praying for healing and deliverance that is asked of them individually, in private, at home or within the group.

What they also have in common is joy and simplicity. One of them smiles less than others because of illness and partial deafness. Their joy comes from their inner being. They hide their trials, and their trials are different. For some they are severe. It is evident they tolerate them well. For some it is the sacrifice of having left behind what they had been doing before, (fortune, glory—for Steve); for others, a lucrative profession, whatever contributed to their human happiness.

Certain of them suffered from opposition. One of them lost her secular friends, who mocked her religious commitments. She lost her husband also. She loved him, but he did not want her to have children and this evoked many problems. He wanted to divorce her. All these problems provoke the Dark Night in one's spiritual life.

The family of one of them denounced her. They suspected her of occultism which we have already seen. Later on we will see Annie's trials.

In re-assessing the whole picture (fruits and hindrances) we recognize the authentic growth of the Body of Christ, as it materializes—there where the Holy Spirit is active, there where the pastoral and freedom co-exist harmoniously, according to grace's organic life. Thus joys and trials thrive as well as the discriminate gifts of God in the service of His Church.

Plurality in unity is a good sign of the Holy Spirit; it is the terrestrial image of the Trinity, where everything is one, except for the distinction of the persons. In Scottsdale, like in all the real Christian communities since the beginning, *Agape* (that is to say Divine Love, charity) unites people and at the same time respects their autonomy. It awakes them to the fact of their own diversity.

2. Can We Talk About Supernatural in Scottsdale?

In the theological sense of the word, supernatural is flowing in torrents in Scottsdale within the group of ten, and extends largely beyond the parish and to the entire country. It is a grace (actuation by God in the most profound depth of one's own soul) and charism (gift of the Holy Spirit for the edification of the Body of Christ, which is the Church). We understand by supernatural, not its extraordinary sense of being prodigious or miraculous, but the ordinary action of grace promised to all by Jesus Christ. There is nothing striking about this grace. But this gift, essentially hidden, is more extraordinary than the miracles, because it is about our spiritual growth, our divinization by the communication of God's very life. Its evidence and its splendor will not be revealed in this life but in the next. In Scottsdale as well as in other places, we discern it by evident signs.

Supernatural is not **miraculous**. The wonder, the inexplicable is but a singular and superficial form of grace.

In the proper sense of the word, supernatural is not a phenomenon which is added on exteriorly to nature like a hat on a head. Supernatural is in the interior of nature. It *accomplishes* the most profound potentialities. So wonderful is this gift that it is not evidently inexplicable. It does not depend on scientific affidavits or proofs, specifically speaking.

Moreover, the Church does not classify saintliness or even mysticism among miracles. Those signs *(sêmeia),* like the Bible states, are not necessarily demonstrable prodigies *(terata).* Exterior display which characterizes the miraculous (astonishing, marvelous) does not always accompany saintliness. Thérèse of Lisieux cultivated saintliness without miracles. She was amused at not finding any (or nearly any) in the life of Our Lady. She rejoiced in contemplating Our Lady as a most ordinary woman. What was wonderful about Mary was her depth, discreet and hidden: faith and charity (love) accordingly. (The exception is the miracle of the Virgin birth which was without display, splendor, or proof). It was with Christ also during His hidden life, in spite of the hypostatic union. The prophet Isaiah announced this in the following austere terms:

He grew up like a sapling before him, like a shoot from the parched earth; There was in him no stately bearing to make us look at him, nor appearance that would attract us to him. He was spurned and avoided by men, a man of suffering, accustomed to infirmity. One of those from whom men hide their faces, spurned, and we held him in no esteem.

Even as many were amazed at him, so marred was his look beyond that of man, and his appearance beyond that of mortals.

(*Isaiah* 53:2-3 and 52:14).

Briefly, "nothing supernatural" was foreseen in the Messiah by the prophet. The Hypostatic Union is at the same time the greatest and the most hidden of all prodigies. It eludes human eyes.

I am not surprised then that the Scottsdale appointed Commission of experts did not discern "miracles," according to the ambiguous terms of the classical question asked in similar cases. If the facts, rapidly examined, appeared to be situated in that particular order of things that are explicable, they nevertheless did not attempt to have explained them either.

"We do not say that it is impossible that there are miracles, we say there is *not enough evidence* to affirm that there are miracles," Fr. Larkin stated very clearly, in *The Catholic Sun,* dated January 18, 1990.

In other words, the Commission did not exclude miracles, not for the future, not even for the present. In the limits of their inquiry, they have not assimiliated sufficient proof to affirm it. They have prudently situated these facts in life's ordinary faith, from a profound divine source, but not miraculous. Likewise, the Transubstantiation, a phenomenon more radically marvelous than a "miracle," is not classified in this category, because the impalpable change is produced beyond the order of "phenomena," at a level which escapes scientific proof.

Therefore, this invites us to interpret the Commission's clear conclusions according to their initial findings as follows:

1. There are normal, supernatural phenomena, theologically of a beautiful quality, like all conversions are. But rarely does a conversion give rise for an inquiry, or find a miracle in the conclusion.

2. It is clear that the events of Scottsdale present some aspects which stem from the ordinary: motions, inspirations, charisms, and other spiritual experiences, not without exterior effects. These unusual facts are situated on a margin where the power of God is affirmed in a verbal way, compelling and sometimes striking. All this remains in semi-darkness *(clair-obscur)*; and even miracles are rarely absolutely evident. It is important to pay attention to this continuity between the ordinary supernatural and the evident signs called "miracles."

Thus, in Scottsdale we might not know just how to support, to praise, to encourage the experience of profound prayer, the contact with God, gift of self, fruitful inititives, which have been developing harmoniously in a remarkable pastoral there.

According to established customs, investigations of apparitions more or less make an abstraction of this essential supernatural. They become polarized on the word "miracle" or the "inexplicable," as if it were the specific object of an investigating Commission.

It is less important to make conclusions regarding miracles than to help and promote actions of grace. A gardener is less pre-occupied with whether spring is a miracle than to assist this dynamic of nature. It is the same in the order of grace, at the level of human liberties stirred by God's free gifts—and this priority is too often neglected.

"It is the saints of the year 2000 that we assassinate," said Daniel Ange, in reference not only to abortions, but to the serious inefficiencies of Christian education. "It is the charisms that we assassinate," we could venture to say today, as well.

Because charisms are delicate plants, they demand the care of a good gardener. They need to be fed with teachings and counsels, endure trials, to be pruned, because they are subject to deviations or to overflow. There is temptation to amplify them unduly, or to prolong them artificially when God's gift is removed.

Finally, visionaries can be susceptible to temptation. Moreover, Satan is particularly active in leading astray (from God) those who could harm the reign of the Prince of this world. Similarly, all such cases demand specific and discreet attention.

But too often, the authentic charisms are opposed, blamed, reprimanded and uprooted as one would do with a poisonous plant.

It is typical during a commission's investigation in cases like these (not those in Scottsdale), to concentrate exclusively on the question of miracle? If the fact could be verified as inexplicable we would say: "It is supernatural." If not (and it is generally the case, sometimes because of lack of time and means taken to sufficiently verify), we will simply say: "supernatural is not established. There is nothing supernatural." And the press translates this quickly as: The Church disqualifies, refuses to accept, condemns, etc., such as in the case of Mejugorje. This fosters confusion, depriving the Church of the normal development of God's gifts in the process. Ambiguous vocabulary and repressive style have often created some malaise in the Church, Medjugorje included. Briefly, there exists in Scottsdale the supernatural of a good quality, where grace is effected and is radiating.

3. Are There Miracles in Scottsdale?

Are the facts of Scottsdale miraculous and inexplicable? It will be asked. This question is not insignificant, for there cannot be abstraction, even if it is premature to answer it.

We can presume, there are, from the healings that are discreetly multiplying. But, they have not been examined enough medically and scientifically. Fr. Spaulding has constantly shown a concern over the supernatural regarding testing and scientific proofs. This gives credit to his pastoral sense.

In such conditions, we can but go along with the prudent formulas of the Commission: no miracle formally established as yet.

But two confusions have to be dissipated in this respect:

A. **Miracles** (supernatural prodigy) can never be proven geometrically. They are like a semi-darkness *(clair-obscur)* with a probable analogy to that which we ordinarily accept in life, (or even in the sciences) without absolute proof. The probabilities which various sciences are satisfied with most often rest on convergences. They are sometimes expressed in statistical terms. It is the same in the spiritual order. God does not constrain man with unimpeachable evidence; He does not provide ready-made proof. There always remains illusion of good faith. And often, criticism renders itself suspicious in regard to God and to the supernatural. Ecclesiastically, the regular procedures are more rigorous than in secular matters, as if we should demand from God some absolute proof. This is not in accord with God's gratuitious style which is nearer to human realities.

B. The **supernatural** and the **prodigious** (the extra-ordinary) are different concepts. Supernatural is much more important than the prodigious but less striking. The divine life, that God gives to man, is a hidden life, but marvelous in the eyes of God Who sees the invisible. That is what will appear as the true miracle in the hereafter. But here on earth it is obscure from man's eyes, more specifically, *from the wise and the learned,* as Jesus says in the Bible (*Matt.* 11:25—*Luke* 10:21). But as seen previously, it could be an eloquent sign, manifested and remarkable. It could be evident for the visionaries and those who live intensively in the grace of God. And this provokes conversions and various positive benefits.

4. An Important Distinction

Beyond the particular problem of Scottsdale, it would be desirable that Investigation Commissions who devote their time to investigating apparitions, be invited to reform and improve the usual concepts which singularly curtail the field of investigations. It is important to ask two very different questions successively.

1. Is it an authentic supernatural phenomenon, remarkable and exemplary?

It is the primordial and principle question, because it concerns the divine life of the Church. At Scottsdale, we can but answer yes to the first question, allowing for some nuances, variations.

2. The divine effectiveness: does it produce the prodigious and inexplicable phenomenon, revealing God's Divine power?

If we are unable to distinguish well these two questions, and unable to sufficiently examine the first (often neglected), we will reach unilateral judgments not too clear regarding God's works, or for man's conduct.

Sometimes, we tend to pronounce a judgment unilaterally and exclusively negative on eminently positive phenomena; and in so doing, instead of recognizing the work of God, we seem to misunderstand it, to scorn or to conceal it. Instead of giving thanks to God, we are distressed and tend to devaluate His gifts. Thus we are of no help in the development of those beautiful plants in the garden of the Holy Spirit. We uproot them.

This often causes conscience problems and unnecessary sufferings, a mess indeed, because those who had found light and conversion in these places do not understand this, nor the hostility.

This harshness ordinarily is based on this test of visionaries: "If the phenomenon comes from God, God will be stronger. If God does not show proof, this is not of God."

This aphorism is misleading. On one hand, it is tempting God—like Georges of Nantes did when he dreamt of dying before the end of the year, instead of Cardinal Lustiger, in order to prove who between the two was wrong. And neither one died.

On the other hand, the visionaries and the charismatics are often fragile human beings. They do not necessarily have the charism of strength. They can lose their bearings, deviate, because of rejection or contradiction. Their difficult situation often calls for a need to be helped, to be assisted, and to be understood.

Severity has dominated during the past half of this century, during which none of the apparitions which happened after Beauraing and Banneux (1933) were recognized. During the first decades after Vatican II, we welcomed enthusiastically and frantically all that came from the world (all secularity— all modernity) under the pretext of being open to the world. It was group dynamism, zen, yoga, transcendental meditation, etc. These hazardous "quests," outside of Christian tradition, were rarely blamed, in spite of evidence of deviations which provoked many priests and lay people to leave the Church, thereby profiting paganism. The Naturalism of theologians was respected, indeed protected. The Supernatural, on the contrary, aroused mistrust and doubt. Negative judgments and repression sometimes fall like the guillotine, when an apparition happens: "it is illusion, illuminism, fanaticism, mass hysteria."

Thus so many Christians welcomed all sorts of ideologies, including those most contrary to Christianity, and this included communism, condemned by Pope Pious XI as intrinsically evil for its atheistic materialism and the warmonger of its fight against classes. We were equally indulgent with the ideological feminism which wants to revive theology in reference to pagan goddesses, to sorceresses, to homosexuality, to re-define the nature of womanhood, and to promote abortion. Many baptized Christian women promoted these laws which not only destroyed babies, but also womens' hearts. Many religious and families have suffered by it; and what to say about the ideologies justifying homosexuality, which were made to accept, to bless, and to even promote this deviation in the seminaries, without consequence. It is curious to see to what point we have encouraged this "overture" to poisonous fruits and to what point we have discouraged or opposed apparitions or charisms responsible for numerous conversions and spiritual developments.

Let us try to distinguish "supernatural" and "miracle." We have to give priority to the essential supernatural and to its fruits, and in cases where we recognize authenticity, make known the proofs of these fruits of grace—those of the miracles.

5. A Recent Evolution Favorable to Apparitions

New norms of the Church have allowed for the progression of this evidence. They formerly treated apparitions with less praise because they are a modest fact in the life of the Church. Now, they tend to welcome and recognize them for what they are. Two institutional phases brought about this evolution:

A. In 1970, Pope Paul VI abolished Canon 1399, § 5, from the ancient Code of Canonical Law which "prohibited books and pamphlets narrating new apparitions, revelations, visions, prophecies and miracles, or else launching new devotions, even though it would be under the pretext that they were Private." (Decree of the *Congregation of the Faith* published in *Acta Apostolicae Sedis*, December 29, 1970, pg. 1186).

This abolition, in conformity with the statute of Christian liberty, had its honor further restored by the Council, putting an end to 40 years of severity due to the accidental confluence of two different and even opposing currents:
—the demythologizing criticism of the left, and,
—the traditional sternness of Cardinal Ottaviani, strict adversary of illuminism, cautious to the point of staying as far away from it as possible.

These contrary diametrical attitudes were added weight against apparitions. Marc Oraison, condemned by Ottaviani for his far left progressiveness, chimed in with him in regard to a highly regarded mystic, Yvonne Aimee de Malestroit. Cardinal Ottaviani had stopped her canonization proceedings. Oraison went beyond, to the point of qualifying her as hysterical, before and against the advice of all the doctors who had examined her. This illustrates how the confluence of the two currents created a joint maximum of discredit for the highest spiritual values.

B. On February 25, 1978, Cardinal Seper, successor to Cardinal Ottaviani as Perfect of the *Congregation of the Catholic Faith*, published the: *New norms on how to proceed in judging presumed apparitions and private revelations.*

This document of four pages has remained confidential until today. But he has sent a "sub secreto" to bishops confronted with this problem. This document inaugurates a new perspective, inspired by Cardinal Seper's pastoral spirit for better acknowledging the gifts of God. He invites us to judge apparitions in the following ways:

That the bishops watch over these phenomena without delay (instead of waiting and keeping their distance according to prevailing custom) and that they should take seriously their responsibilities. They should judge if there is doctrinal or moral deviation, and in this case, that they should intervene rapidly to put an end to the error. But if the phenomena is sound and if its fruits are good, that they assume the cult; because the faithful should be guided by the Church and not abandoned to the risk of deviation.

It is this favorable hypothesis, and after this only, that they without haste examine if there is an extraordinary phenomena that can be authenticated as a miracle.

In short, the official document distinguishes two points:

• The recognition of the ordinary supernatural: prayer, spiritual fervor, good fruits (and of course absence of deception or illusion).

• Recognition of the miraculous characteristic, if it happens.

Normally, in the first instance there is recognition of a "cult" and pilgrimages. The bishop would take it in stride prudently, without having to make a judgment as to the miracle. This is what happened in San Nicolás, Kibeho, and Akita, where the bishops encouraged the devotion. The same occurred in Scottsdale, where the question remains open and could lead to ulterior investigations. Nothing is closed.

6. Blessings for Scottsdale

We can give thanks for Scottsdale in many ways. One of the prejudices against apparitions has been: "Why is it always the Blessed Virgin who appears, and what becomes of Jesus in things like that?"

In Scottsdale, Our Lord is apparently manifesting Himself even more than Our Blessed Mother (as proven proportionately through the statistics of the messages), and she manifests herself in order to lead the people to Jesus. Truthfully, it is in conformity with her role.

Biblical revelation formerly seemed an opponent to apparitions, which seemed to cast a shadow. At Scottsdale, like in San Nicolás and elsewhere, the apparitions do not divert one from the Bible, but lead one to it. Rather, the visionaries and others bring forth hunger for the Word of God through their witness. We can give thanks for the Christian exigency which directs the visionaries' lives, and supports the spiritual growth, in the parish and beyond.

We must also give thanks for the "pastoral sense" which permitted this harmonious convergence of the gifts of the Holy Spirit and this freedom. The visionaries are often disturbed by what is happening to them. "Am I going crazy?" asked many of them in Scottsdale. When they were abandoned, not without peril and with the help of the devil's temptations, Fr. Jack Spaulding conveniently reassured and guided them. After having ascertained the convergence and the theological authenticity of the graces, he brought the visionaries together in order for them to share their experiences (beginning of September 1988).

At the same time, he has maintained a firm discretion. The parish was basically not aware of the events previously unfolding. The movement had to progress from the interior, under the auspices of the Holy Spirit, without the display of publicity. Obedience to the bishop was within that bound.

This discretion had the advantage of preventing a danger that is not negligible. In such cases, the extraordinary events rally part of the parishioners but rebuff the rest. The first group forge ahead while the others contest. The parish is divided. This has happened in the *Charismatic Renewal,* Protestant or Catholic, from the very early stages.

Fr. Spaulding knew how to ally listening and openheartedness to God, discernment and spiritual direction, pastoral prudence and obedience, often difficult in matters like these, because the rules coming from the exterior often impede the movement of the Holy Spirit and the enthusiasm that is aroused.

The just articulation of these gifts with the generous response of the visionaries, and the prudence of the pastor, provided the counter-balance and the abundance of the fruits.

7. Pitfalls and Risks

Discernment then seems positive. But it is a beginning, and what will follow is not easy, because the pitfalls and the temptations are numerous in such a case.

The visionaries are very different. It is not easy for them to maintain unity among themselves and with the pastor. They risk disintegration. The devil, whose name signifies division, tempts by priority on this point.

The exceptional graces are difficult to assume well. They are heavy to carry where the appeals of the faithful to the ministry of healing and other demands are multiplied.

Perseverance in these difficult situations is also a problem. Sometimes the workings of the Holy Spirit fail for that reason. Nothing is more difficult for us than perseverance. Time is triumphant only to the humble effort of the daily occurrence.

The scientific study of ecstasy and presumed miracles (notably healings) is, without a doubt, desirable for a better discernment of the supernatural; but spiritual development must be of the utmost importance. It is the priority of all priorities.

8. Three Objections

A critic of Scottsdale listed three objections to me of the messages and lessons in the passages of Vol. I of the *"I Am Your Jesus of Mercy"* books. His objections are as follows:

1. (Pg. 50): "The Trinity is presented as a 'symbol' and not as a 'mystery.' It would be a body. This text eliminates the Trinity, at the same time symbolizing and materializing it as a body."

I believe this is a misunderstanding of the text. To start with, the "symbol" of the Trinity is a triangle. It invites us to go beyond this preposterous geometric symbol to a living revelation of the Three Persons who share the same Being and communicate the same life to us.

Thanks to this communication, the Trinity is perceived as a living unity in which we participate—like a social body. Jesus explains as much so well in John 17, when He says to The Father:

*so that they may all be one, as you, Father, are
in me and I in you, that they also may be in us,
that the world may believe that you sent me.*

The word "body" signifies this vital mystical unity, quasi
organic. It is not a "mystery" in the sense that this word
would signify an obscurity, incomprehensible and not
penetrable, because by communion, faith does penetrate this
great Mystery like a great light.

2. (Pg. 67): "The Cross is presented as a symbol and not
   as a mystery."

If we read the text well, we will understand that the Cross
is a symbol of God's love, and that at the same time, it is
a profound and sorrowful reality. Here again, the obscurity
of the mystery of God's suffering in person, which is beyond
our comprehension, becomes a living light which enables us
to penetrate the text and its sense.

3. (Pg. 105): "This 'anniversary message' seems to focus on
   Gianna's marriage. It has since ended in a divorce and has
   been annulled by the Church. Therefore, it was evidently
   erroneous."

Nothing indicates that this message was for Gianna. It
encourages all married couples to place Jesus in the heart
of their home. Gianna, to whom I had submitted these three
objections, sent me her responses. They are worth noting
here.

(Response)

   I The explanation of the Trinity is as follows:
      "One Body" is a metaphor and it symbolizes the organic
   unit at a Divine spiritual level. It does not mean there
   is any material in God.
      "Symbol": Jesus does NOT say the Trinity is a symbol,
   but that the triangle is the symbol of the Trinity. The triangle is the traditional symbol and needs no explanation.
   The Trinity is not a symbol.

"Mystery": Jesus uses mystery in two different ways and in a different sense. There are two meanings.

1. Mystery means something incomprehensible.
2. Normally speaking, a mystery is something that we can know more and more about, but cannot fully understand.

The Trinity is strictly a mystery as something totally incomprehensible as stated above. Yet, Jesus also says that it is not a mystery in that we know more and more about living in unity tied to the oneness of the Trinity, even though we cannot fully understand it.

II The Cross (pg. 67) itself is not a mystery. The death of Jesus is the mystery. Death for our salvation is the mystery. The Cross itself is a program, a way to live.

III Marriage (pg. 105). I personally do not know about that message. Nowhere in the message is my name mentioned. It was a message for all married people who place Jesus at the center of their lives, as I understand it.

The lesson on the cross raised another ojection, namely that Jesus states "the cross will not be painful." Yet, we know that suffering is painful.

Yes, but like most prophecies, it implies an exaggeration to appreciate two points:

• Jesus suffered more than we do and His redemptive suffering gives a grace stronger than suffering.
• This grace does not suppress suffering, but gives peace and strength allowing us to overcome suffering with a smile. Susan Evans and Gianna know this well.

CHAPTER 9

Radiance of Scottsdale

1. Testimonies

"My niece, Lyn and her husband Eddie were here in Scottsdale about two weeks ago, just to pray. Their specific intention in coming here was to have someone pray over them. What happened besides was that they experienced a real conversion of the heart. They loved everything here. 'My best vacation,' said Eddie to me.

"And all they did was pray. They are thinking of returning to St. Maria Goretti for their next vacation. They would like to make the retreat for young adults. Moreover they are planning a pilgrimage to Medjugorje. Thank you for welcoming them (. . .) I am quoting a part of the note that they have sent to me (communicated):

" 'The love and the energy that radiates from the church of St. Maria Goretti is what all churches should have. Father Jack, Father Eric, the young adults and all in St. Maria Goretti are so open, so loving! This pilgrimage has really changed our lives.' " (Letter to Pat Houghton of St. Maria Goretti Parish—March 22, 1990).

"My wife and I, along with three other couples, spent a few days in Scottsdale and attended the 5:30 p.m. Mass in the parish church of St. Maria Goretti. I realize it is not logical to jump to conclusions after a Mass of 60 minutes. But in my opinion, this parish has the best 'esprit de corps' that I have ever observed. It is also obvious to me that Fr. Jack Spaulding is the catalyst. If we had more priests like him, we would have a Catholic population of at least 100 million in our country.

"He can say more in 10 minues than many can say in 45 minutes. This he does without notes, without hesitation and with the most sincerity. All those who participated at this Mass did it with respect and this includes altar servers, ushers, eucharistic ministers, lectors, deacons, choir, unrivalled. (. . .) It was the most marvelous light of our five days in Scottsdale. You are lucky to have a man of this caliber as pastor of St. Maria Goretti." (Hal F. Tehan, Executive Director of the *Catholic Foundation* to Bishop T. J. O'Brien.)

"My friend and I, the two of us in our thirties, were visiting my family in Scottsdale last year. We went to the 10:45 a.m. Mass on Sunday, and we have not been able to stop talking about it. It was the most inspiring service that we have ever encountered. The music, the singing, the sermon, everything was alive. We were very impressed with the gospel reading, recited from memory and explained very profoundly." (Letter from B. R.—March 1, 1990.)

2. Spiritual Fruits

The fruits of Scottsdale are evident. They are due to the spiritual growth of the visionaries, their generous fidelity the past four years, and the unfolding of their charisms, which are also fruitful.

They are due to the radiance of the events in the parish, and beyond the parish, as the success of the messages books indicate.

They are due to the conversions, the healings, and the radiance that increases in the wake of the events.

In regard to this last point, since it is easier to talk about the deceased, let us invoke the case of Diane Sauerman only, a member of St. Maria Goretti parish.

She died on Divine Mercy Sunday, April 7, 1991. She was stricken with cancer which had been in remission several times but which flared up again in 1988. Her suffering and prayers touched many people.

During these hard last years, Diane went from conversion to conversion in a profound way. Those who would come to attend to her would go back with a new peace of Jesus. One of the messages given to the prayer group was very encouraging to her in this period of purification. (We will find other testimonies of this radiance on another page).

3. Healings

But are there healings in Scottsdale? Many are receiving healings and give thanks to God, but no records have been filed from which to draw convincing conclusions. Here are a few cases gathered in September 1991, in the course of an investigation by Bill Reck.

Norbert Rehmann

Norbert Rehmann, 68 years old, was an active member of St. Maria Goretti Parish for many years. In 1980, he underwent serious heart surgery in Cleveland, Ohio. It involved the replacement of the mitral valve.

In 1987, there was a second operation at *St. Mary's of Arizona Heart Institute.* Dr. Dietrick had replaced the aeorta valve. During the next several years, his condition deteriorated. In March of 1990, Dr. Kashmir, Cardiologist at the *Mayo Clinic* of Scottsdale confirmed that the valves were now leaking and that the aeorta valve had torn loose. Both had to be replaced. His prognosis for successful surgery was extremely limited. The decision was left up to Norbert. He accepted and the operation was arranged for the first week in April 1990. An echo-gram procedure had confirmed the severity of his state.

Norbert and Marielle had been active members of the Thursday evening prayer group, and one evening during prayer for healing he presented himself to be prayed over. Fr. Jack invited him to come back to be prayed over until which time he would be operated on.

At the *Mayo Clinic,* north of Scottsdale, during the first week of April 1990, as he was being surgery-prepped, x-rays, tests, etc., he was praying: "Jesus, help me," and he could feel His presence very profoundly. They had started the anesthesia...

He woke up in his room. No surgical procedures had been performed.

"Everything is fine," the doctor came to tell him. "Did you not do it because you felt I could not afford it," he asked the doctor.

"No."

"Then why haven't you done it?"

"The valves are all perfect. I have no explanation for this. You might as well go home. There's simply nothing wrong with your heart."

Mr. Rehmann was asked to come back in one week for a further examination and evaluation. The results confirmed a totally and completely normal heart condition.

It was not to be the only time Norbert Rehmann would experience such gifts of a supernatural nature. During the summer of 1990, he had tests performed to determine the cause of additional discomfort of the upper torso. The results were not positive. Cancer (Melanoma) was the diagnosis. While vacationing in Michigan in the fall of 1990, Mr. Rehmann went through a bone marrow test at the *Burns Clinic* in Petosky, Michigan. The results confirmed the original diagnosis and initial treatments of chemotherapy were begun.

The Rehmanns returned to Scottsdale where Norbert went to see Fr. Jack for prayer and counseling. Prayers for healing took place in the parish. In late 1990 Norbert went to the *Mayo Clinic* (Scottsdale) for additional tests under the direction of Dr. Reeder, an Oconologist. The tests proved to be completely negative. No cancer was apparent.

Mr. Rehmann's trials still continue. In October of 1991, while again vacationing at their cottage in Michigan, Norbert was admitted to the *Burns Clinic* suffering from massive swelling and partial fibrosis of the lungs. Fluids were not being dispersed through his system and was affecting the kidneys. The diagnosis was extreme—congestive heart failure.

Interestingly, it **was not** the heart valves which had been inserted previously that caused the heart failure. They were functioning. Instead it was massive heart failure originating from the tricuspid valve and affecting the lower chamber. During these trying hours Mr. Rehmann reported seeing a vision of the crucified Christ at his hospital room window. The future was extremely bleak for him.

In November 1991 Mr. Rehmann had recovered enough to be returned to his home in Scottsdale, and was again admitted to the *Mayo Clinic.* Dr. Sara Mambi, a heart specialist, confirmed his condition, further advising that his age and condition would not support a needed heart and lung transplant. Further, even if available, such transplants would be preferentially given to a younger patient since Mr. Rehmann was now 69 years old. The prognosis was affirmed by Drs. Barnett, Lee and Eckstein at the clinic. In January 1992, and again in March, Norbert Rehmann was re-admitted to the *Mayo Clinic* for progressively deteriorating systems of the same congestive heart failure. In early May of 1992, (the time of this printing), Mr. Rehmann has returned home still thwarting a fate prescribed for him many years earlier.

In speaking with Marielle Rehmann the first week of May 1992 (at St. Maria Goretti) it is not difficult to assess the basis for their faith. Marielle, like her husband, is a person committed to a strong prayer regime. In fact, she has often devoted many hours to prayer for healing, for many people, not just her husband. Combined with the additional prayer support of Fr. Jack and the special group at St. Maria Goretti, Mr. Rehmann's battle continues.

Dale Nagle

On the Monday of Holy Week, March 22, 1989, Dale Nagle, then 55 years of age, suffered a sudden and massive stroke. The only prior symptom was a strong headache the previous day. He was rushed to *Scottsdale Memorial Hospital.* On Wednesday, March 24, he had slipped into a coma. By Good Friday, his condition was determined to be fatal.

He was diagnosed as "brain dead." His life continued only through the use of life support systems.

Due to the severity and strange aspects of the sudden stroke and heart attack, his wife, Marilyn, consented to an autopsy to determine if any future hereditary aspects could be diagnosed, with respect to the children. The only possible continuation of life for Dale Nagle would be as a vegetable. On Easter Sunday 1989, the visionary Gianna received a message from Our Lord: *Mr. Nagle is only sleeping; it is time to awaken him.*

Gianna did not know who Mr. Nagle was, and reported the message to Fr. Jack Spaulding. Gianna went to Scottsdale Memorial Hospital with Stefanie Staab and Fr. Jack and Carol Ameche at the same time that numerous parishioners and other members of the family were assembled for the last hours of Mr. Nagle's life. They cleared the room for private prayer. The patient's condition remained unchanged that day. On the Tuesday after Easter, suddenly his reflexes started. On Thursday, movement and sight returned and he recognized his wife and extended his hand to her.

Mr. Nagle's health had been perfect prior to the sudden stroke. It could not be medically predictable, nor could the hospital staff offer any explanation as to his sudden recovery. Today Dale Nagle is ambulatory, functions on his own. He, who was totally paralyzed and had lost the use of speech and of hearing, now hears perfectly well and has regained much of his speech. He still feels a little weakness on the right side as he walks. But since October 20, 1991 he has regained complete autonomy.

Doctor X

Dr. X, a well-known doctor in his city, a practicing Catholic, who desires to remain anonymous for professional reasons, benefited thusly from the charisms of the parish of St. Maria Goretti.

On July 31, 1989, at 3:40 p.m., he had a severe car accident. He barely escaped death. Six broken ribs, as well as the clavicle, along with a number of hematomas. He was transported to *Saint Joseph Hospital* in the intensive care unit. His state cast doubt as to his professional future, which demands full energy and dexterity of his hands. Receiving an inspiration, which he could not explain, he requested that Gianna Talone be called in. Gianna is the coordinator of the pharmaceutical department of the hospital where he was being treated. She came discreetly to pray for him. A few hours later, he was transferred from ICU to a regular hospital room, for observation. No surgery was necessary.

Today, he has returned to his normal activities. His recuperation is complete without any deficiencies. In spite of his scientific mind, he is convinced of supernatural intervention. Daily rosary is part of his answer.

Nancy Adams

Nancy Adams is a middle-aged housewife and mother, and an active member of St. Maria Goretti Parish.

On July 19, 1991, she had a mammogram, confirming a lump in the breast. It is important to note that these x-rays were taken at 8:00 in the morning. She was the first patient scheduled that day. There was no chance for a mix-up with any other x-ray. The x-ray results revealed a definite mass indicating surgical removal. Exploratory procedures were completed.

Nancy returned home waiting further word from her doctor who was already setting up the surgery for July 25, 1991 at *Maricopa County Hospital*. During this difficult period of waiting, everything was going wrong. She sought spiritual help from a friend, a radiologist. She asked that the date of the operation be postponed to August 13, 1991 at 8:00 a.m. She never bothered to confirm the fact that the tumor was cancerous and instead used the two week interval to seek the will of the Lord and to ask Him to walk with her. The prayer groups at St. Maria Goretti responded to her need along with numerous parishioners. Specific prayers for healing were offered at the Thursday night liturgy.

On August 13, 1991 at 6:30 a.m., the scheduled taxi arrived to transport her to *Maricopa County Hospital.* Prior to her relocation in Scottsdale, Nancy Adams had worked as an operating room coordinator, on the east coast. She knew well the procedure. She was immediately taken to radiology where it was confirmed to her that the tumor was definitely Carsinoma and that the cancer was at an advanced state. She states that she then felt the very profound presence of Our Lord. Her only response was: "It's OK. He will walk with me through this."

A new x-ray was taken to determine any change of the tumor during the previous three week period. The anesthiologist and operating room staff were present and prepared. Nothing happened.

For thirty minutes she sat and waited. An operating room nurse then came in and told her: "We have to talk to your doctor." After an additional 30 minutes, several doctors appeared. "Nancy, we can't find your tumor. It's gone," stated the doctor.

"Did I really ever have one," she asked?

"Absolutely," he said, "but it's simply no longer there. I can't explain it."

"I told him how many prayers were being offered for me and asked: 'Are you saying it's a miracle then?' "

He answered: "Yes, I can't explain it any other way."

Nancy Adams was then sent home. Further tests revealed no trace of any cancerous tumor.

Lindsay Brand

Lindsay Brand was born on October 7, 1985. At the age of two she appeared to be becoming lethargic, with vision problems and swelling of the neck and head. Her pediatrician, Dr. Duane Wooten, a highly successful and respected doctor, was consulted. Additional tests were performed at *Children's Hospital,* a unit of the *Good Samaritan Hospital* of Phoenix, Arizona.

The diagnosis was extremely grave. A very large tumor was present and had wrapped itself around the brain stem of this child. The diagnosis was made on August 17, 1988. Emergency surgery was scheduled for two days later, August 19, 1988. It was to be an operation that could take ten hours and was to be performed by Dr. Harold Rekate, Neurosurgeon. Since severe hydro-cephalus was present, Lindsay was given a 50% chance of surviving the surgery. Her chances of survival after the surgery were reduced from there. She was given a projected five year life span, at best. The surgery was successful in that Lindsay survived and 95% of the tumor had been removed. Chemotherapy did not shrink the remaining tumor, inaccessible during surgery. A subsequent scan showed the tumor remnant still present. A milo-gram scan indicated that part of the remnant tumor had slipped to the spine and immediate radiation treatment was required—additional suffering for a two year old who had already undergone extensive medical treatment at this point.

Lindsay's mother, Penny Brand, experienced a strong conversion during this period. She had fallen away from her faith and saw, through Lindsay's trials, redemptive suffering of her own. Following the surgery and initial treatments, Lindsay's needs were brought to Anne Ross, Gianna Talone, Fr. Spaulding and the prayer group at St. Maria Goretti. Penny also sought out Jack Ahern, who leads a prayer group at neighboring St. Agnes Parish. It is a group that specifically dedicated itself to healing prayer.

Following prayer sessions over Lindsay, Lindsay made mention of the "Holy Spirit" an entity entirely unknown to a three year old child. Lindsay began her own prayers. A scan in the fall of 1989 had revealed there was no change in Lindsay's condition and that the tumor remnants were still viable. Chemotherapy had begun in September of 1988, with no effect. In February 1989, radiation treatment had begun. Scans in May and August of 1989 revealed no change in her condition. On October 12, 1989, Lindsay's needs were presented to those mentioned above for prayer for healing.

On November 5, 1989, another scan was performed on Lindsay. The results were suddenly clear. Treatments were halted by her mother. In February 1990, Lindsay was given another scan. The results were clear. No tumor could be found. Today, Lindsay functions as a normal five year old child. Even her hair is returning.

Lindsay's father is of the Jewish faith and does not really accept the possibility of any healing.

Patricia Simko

Pat Simko is a 48 year old mother of two living in Los Altos, California, some thirty miles from San Francisco. In 1987 she appeared to be in perfect health. Early in 1988, in response to groin pains, she was diagnosed as having a very severe cancer (melanoma) of the left groin area. The tumor was large. On February 22, 1988, surgery was performed on the advice of her doctor, Dr. Lessin. The surgery took place at the *Kaiser Cancer Institute* under the direction of Dr. Stefanko. The results seemed positive and Pat Simko was told to hope for the best.

Mrs. Simko, a Catholic, knew of the value of prayer and along with her mother and other friends, began concerted prayer effort that the cancer would not return. Included in this effort was Dr. Bonnie Fiori, a psychologist and close friend of Pat Simko. Bonnie Fiori took the petition of her friend to Medjugorje and returned to Medjugorje in late spring of 1990, a trip Bonnie and Pat would repeat.

The trip to Medjugorje in spring of 1990 included dark overtones for the cancer had returned. In May of 1990 a large mass was discovered again in the groin area of Pat Simko. This time the prognosis was somber. It was inoperable and she was given a 30% chance of survival. The only alternative available was whatever relief chemotherapy could provide. To complicate matters more, Pat's left leg began to swell up horribly. Nymph lodes had been removed in the previous surgery and the drainage system had been affected. Draining and infection were accumulating in the leg. Chemotherapy was begun in May of 1990 and visits to the *UCLA Medical Center* confirmed the seriousness of her condition.

In 1989, Bonnie Fiori had traveled to St. Maria Goretti

Parish on a pilgrimage led by Bob Adler from Palo Alto, CA. They returned again in 1990. Again, prayer was offered for Pat Simko. In September of 1990, Bonnie asked Pat Simko to join them on another trip to Scottsdale. She accepted. The chemotherapy was going unexplainably well and the tumor had suddenly shrunk dramatically. She was not affected by the treatment—no sickness—and even did not lose her hair.

At Scottsdale, Gianna asked Bob Adler to have Pat Simko sit next to her at the Thursday night prayer service. During the 3rd decade of the Rosary, Gianna suddenly fell to her knees. The apparition was taking place. Pat Simko stared at Gianna in amazement and at the apparent apparition she was seeing. She was overwhelmed. Following the liturgy, additional individual prayer was offered by Gianna and the other members of the group at St. Maria Goretti for Pat's needs. Later that evening, Gianna told Pat that: "Our Lady was laughing at you because of the look of amazement on your face. She also gave you a special blessing."

In February of 1991 the chemo treatments stopped. The tumor was gone and her leg returned to near normal conditions. Her doctors were unable to explain the rather dramatic extensive success of the chemotherapy, if in fact it was the therapy that had been the cause of her recovery. They sent her to see Doctor Morton, head of the Melanoma Research Department of the *John Wayne Cancer Clinic* (UCLA). He was unable to give any adequate explanation of the dramatic change in Pat Simko's condition.

For her, it is a miracle: a supernatural intervention. She does not know if we should attribute the miracle to Our Lady of Medjugorje or Our Lady of Joy venerated in St. Maria Goretti Church. It does not matter, she is the same Lady. Pat simply offers thanks.

Barbara Kutz

Let us cite briefly one of the numerous thank you letters that Fr. Spaulding received.

"In September 1990, while I was on tour visiting Arizona

(Grand Canyon) and California, I visited Scottsdale. At that time, I was suffering from severe arthritis and high blood pressure. I also was having reactions to the many medications which I was taking. I would spend many days crying. I would ask God to come and get me if He could not heal me, because life had become unbearable. I spent three days in a hospital in Hemet, California, where my husband's sister resides. On November 1, I was able to leave the hospital for Scottsdale, where I arrived 15 minutes before they started the rosary. A friend had given me a book of the messages which had given me a great deal of peace and joy.

"Since that day, November 1, I do not suffer from arthritis and I do not take any prescribed medication for this illness. I had diminished the dosage of the medication for my high blood pressure on the advice of Dr. Mello. Then, in January, I woke up with normal pressure and I stopped taking the prescribed medications: Tenormin, Esidrix and some time later, Apresolone. I also have stopped taking heart medication. I do not take anymore medication for inflammation of the thyroid gland. And, I do not know if I will continue not taking any medication since God has healed everything. Thanks be to God for this miracle, which has changed my life. I did not understand the role of Our Blessed Mother. I finally understood by reading about the messages and going to that parish. I now have a great confidence in her intercession."

This letter was attached to many affidavits, notably one from Dr. Michael Porvaznik of Oakville, Missouri. He stated:

"Mrs. Barbara Kutz, 53 years old, has been treated by me for three years for a long history of severe hypertension and arthritis. Numerous medications had been prescribed for her in order to control her problems.

"Since a few weeks ago, she has practically no arthritis pain and her blood pressure has returned to normal without taking medication."

Mr. Ronald Dane

Ron Dane, 49 years of age, married, is a resident of southern California. In April of 1991, following months of extreme intestinal discomfort, he was diagnosed as having Crohn's Disease. Crohn's Disease is a vicious attack on the intestines. It causes sores and infections in the intestinal walls, eventually preventing the natural function of the intestines. A surgical colostomy is oftentimes the result. The disease is further complicated by the fact that natural healing of these sores and infections can often cause further lesions to form which can only be completely healed through surgical means. The diagnosis and subsequent treatment was done by Dr. Mennon in Apple Valley, California. Mr. Dane was informed that surgery could not cure the problem.

Ron Dane is a very active Catholic who is heavily committed to prayer. His prayer of petition, however, has always been for others, not himself. At the end of August, 1991, Ron and his wife went to the SCRC convention in California. There, he was prayed over by Gianna Talone from St. Maria Goretti Parish, who attended the conference and was a major part of the prayer sessions. Mr. Dane stated, "I felt the complete presence of Jesus when I looked in her eyes as she started to pray over me." He rested in the Spirit.

On October 10, 1991, he had a very bad attack and was put in the hospital. A scopotomy was performed and he was told the disease had seemed to go into some remission, and that because of that, it would be time to perform surgery to repair the fissures left. He was told there was only a 5% chance of healing on its own. Mr. Dane then sought a second opinion from a surgeon and specialist in this disease (Dr. Rutledge—Apple Valley, CA.) who advised caution as to the surgery and the possible ramifications. After two days of discernment, Ron Dane notified the doctor of his decision not to have any surgery performed.

In early November 1991, Ron and his wife made a painful trip to Scottsdale, and St. Maria Goretti. While there, he also visited Estela Ruiz, a visionary in South Phoenix. At St.

Maria Goretti additional prayers were offered and, in praying over him, Fr. Jack Spaulding told Ron: "Pray for your own healing, not just for others. Pray like Jesus and Mary are sitting right in front of you and talk to them."

Upon his return to California, and after several surprisingly good, pain-free weeks, Ron Dane again met with Drs. Mennon and Rutledge. Their examination revealed that the healing was surprisingly complete on its own and that no surgery would be needed. Mr. Dane then went to Loma Linda Hospital in San Bernadino, California for further opinion and tests. So complete was the remission and healing that the medical staff at Loma Linda Hopsital were hesitant to even state that he had experienced Crohn's Disease.

In January of 1992, Mr. Dane recognized the absence of pain and had total intestinal control. He continues to work at his profession. On April 10, 1992, in a conversation with Bill Reck of the Riehle Foundation, he confirmed that he is no longer on any medication or medical treatment, and further, all special diets have been eliminated. He expressed absolute assurance that he is the beneficiary of a special gift from God, while recognizing that medical proof will probably never substantiate it.

4. The Messages Bear Their Fruits

The three volumes of the messages *"I Am Your Jesus of Mercy"* have been read by tens of thousands of people and many have sent their acknowledgment to the publisher. The Riehle Foundation in turn can attest to this by the immense amount of mail they have received, manifesting their fruits. Here are some brief extracts:

"I found so much tranquility and peace in reading this book, which my cousin has given me. Send me ten more so that I can give them to all the members of my family. We have to read and re-read these messages in order to understand the reality of it all." (M. C., NM.)

"I read and re-read, daily, your book *I Am Your Jesus of Mercy* which one of my friends had lent me. I was very taken and inspired." (R. M. V., TX, September 28, 1990.)

"This book touched me. I have never read one so sweet and gentle." (V. F., MD, May 30, 1990.)

"The other evening, I started to read this book: most inspiring. I have never read one like it. I cannot describe the effect it had on me." (T. P. V., NJ, 1990.)

"This book brings a great spiritual uplifting. In reading it, I felt He was talking directly to me. My life really needed it." (D. D. B., TX, April 19, 1990.)

"I cried when our deacon read some passages from this book. Send me two more." (D. P., NY, June 4, 1990.)

"It is the best religious book I have ever read." (D. C., Lauderdale, FL, March 21, 1990.)

"It is the most powerful book we ever have read." (J. & B. D., Miami, FL, March 13, 1990.)

"These books have greatly impressed and inspired me." (Sr. L. T., CSSC, Holland, PA.)

"These books have been a blessing for me." (B. N., Fredericksburg, VA.)

"I had spent a long time studying the Bible, but never have I grasped the meaning like now in this book. I thank God for having given us this marvelous book." (From a Mexican-American [Latino] community.)

"My mother died of cancer; this was hard on me. She was a marvelous woman. . .I now read these books and they have been comforting to me: *I Am Your Jesus of Mercy I* and *II*. Please send me 5 more. We are all going to visit St. Maria Goretti Church (my father, my 2 sisters and my brother)."

"This book radiates ecumenism," a non-Catholic writes: "A friend gave me a copy of this book and we think it is a very good tool to use to live a true Christian life." (L.K., Green Bay, WI.)

"Send me 4 copies of the three books. I have read already the first two but I have given them to some non-Catholic friends who have accepted this book better than those I had given before about Our Lady. My nephew (15) wrote to me: 'I've never found such a good book.' Many attest to the fact that this book has changed their lives. It has greatly contributed to my spiritual life." (M. P., Hopedate, MA, January 16, 1991.)

"From the very first reading of this book, it was helpful in a difficult situation that I had with my adult son. I learned to be merciful toward him like I would want Jesus to have Mercy on him. It was a tremendous lesson, which I needed. Send me five books." (E. J. G., SC, December 8, 1990.)

"I read each day the words of Jesus and Mary. They help me to change my life. I am so excited with the change" (in my life).

Others follow a discernment more hesitant, more critical, as the following example:

Father Michael Sparough, a Jesuit priest, wrote a long dissertation on his investigation and impressions titled: *A Skeptic Goes to Scottsdale.* The skeptic armed with modernism, respectful of the Commission's judgment and their negative opinion (formulas) regarding the characteristics of miracles, was impressed by the quality of the visionaries, of the prayer, certain signs that defy all demonstration: He had his stay at St. Maria Goretti unexpectedly extended due to a very rare fog that suddenly cancelled his flight out. He states:

"I was in no way prepared to say definitively that the apparitions are true. To do it would have been usurping the authority of the Church. It is up to the bishop to decide officially if the apparitions are inspired or fraudulent. But I do not have to wait for the Commission's investigation results to understand that the grace of God has entered thusly in my life. . .I know that Our Lord and His Mother have once again touched my heart like in Medjugorje. Grace has flowed toward me through the Word of God, the Eucharist, and Reconciliation, through the visionaries, the staff and the parishioners. . . . I am starting to understand more clearly the dynamics of interrelation among the young adults and with Father Jack. It is not that I loved everything that I heard and saw. . . . Prophecies, apparitions, visions and locutions are gifts from God in the service of the Church, they are not *proofs*. But God Almighty and all Loving is working with these young people and their pastor, remolding their hearts. What continues to convince me of the validity of their alleged mystical walk, is that it is a life of faith 'extraordinarily ordinary.' It is with great humility that they are struggling to learn, by their own faults, and to continue to carry their cross and to follow Our Lord.

"According to Father Thomas Keating, in his book: *Open Mind Open Heart,* communications of this sort are probably authentic 80% and not authentic 20%; hence the necessity of a well-applied and attentive discernment. Life in the parish of St. Maria Goretti is not confined to the visions and locutions, which could be terminated tomorrow without which, faith would not cease to grow. The Eucharist is the heartbeat of this parish. In November 1991, they celebrated at St. Maria Goretti 10,000 hours of perpetual adoration of the Holy Sacrament.

"Many areas in America are in a spiritual desert. The presence of Our Lord and Our Lady in Scottsdale is an oasis in this desert, but we need to have eyes of faith in order to distinguish a true vision from a mirage. *"Blessed are those who have not seen and yet believe,"* said Jesus to His disciples

(*John* 20:29). "In the parish of St. Maria Goretti, I have seen nothing so supernatural that it would eliminate all doubts. But I have confidence in the truth that sings in my heart, and I have confidence in the people whom I have met there. Their testimony was instrumental in revealing Jesus and His Mother to me." (J. Michael Sparough, SJ, November 21, 1991.)

Rev. Tim Sockol (Florida) sent correspondence to The Riehle Foundation concerning a number of conversions directly attributable to the *"I Am Your Jesus of Mercy"* books. In one such letter he states:

"Only this month a couple returned to Church after reading these books. Their marriage was on the brink of divorce. Both husband and wife were at Mass two weeks ago for the first time in years. The husband, who was not willing to come to try to reconcile the marriage, is now sending copies of these books to members of his family. This is typical of the type of experiences the books have brought."

"There were days when the book would just keep 'calling' me, so to speak, and the particular lesson that I was led to read was right on the mark for something I was going through at the time. He is so good to us and loves us so much. Praise God!" (D. M. S., NJ, March 1990.)

"This book has blessed my days. I thank you for your efforts. When Mary said 'conversion,' she also saw to it that there was the means to help strengthen that conversion. Thank you for saying yes to *"I Am Your Jesus of Mercy!"* (M. E. J., WY, October 1991.)

"We have Volume I and II, and words cannot express the help and inspiration they contain! It's as if Our Lord and Blessed Mary are trying to give people one last chance before it's too late. We will read them over and over and try our best to practice and live what they teach." (J. R. Jr., FL, November 1991.)

(From a non-Catholic) "My books were given to me by a Catholic friend and my life has truly been blessed by them. A great deal of sickness and trouble has been in our family the last 3 years and I felt nearly at the end of endurance when I received these. I've placed all of these things in His hands." (I. M., IN).

The summation of all these glowing responses to the books could be summed up in the words of a letter by Fr. Jim Willig (Cincinnati, OH), who spent a week at St. Maria Goretti in 1991. He states in his letter:

"I made a week's retreat recently at St. Maria Goretti Parish, and during my retreat I had the privilege of meeting privately and individually with several of the young visionaries who claim to be seeing and/or hearing Our Blessed Mother on a regular basis.

"Initially, I was a little skeptical of these apparitions, but soon after meeting with the visionaries, I found them to be psychologically, theologically and spiritually very sound. In fact, I was amazed at their insights and wondered how they could have come to this spiritual wisdom having had no prior theological or scriptural training. There was no way for me to verify their experiences but almost immediately I found myself intuitively believing them.

"Perhaps more important, after listening to them I felt very drawn to Our Blessed Mother in my own prayer time. I truly believe, as they state, that Mary wants to be our mother and lead us to her Son, Jesus. And as I prayed with Mary, I experienced her presence with me in a way that I have never before experienced in my life. I felt her great love and support. I felt that Jesus was giving His Mother to me just as He had given her to His disciple, John.

"Again, there is no way I can verify this, even

for myself. All I know is that even now, long after my retreat has ended, I still sense Mary's presence with me throughout the day, especially when I invite her to join me as I pray. I have now consecrated my life and my priesthood to Mary. She is the woman that I always suspected I needed in my life."

Conclusion

These are but a few of the testimonies received at the Riehle Foundation. They have been unable to keep track of all these documents. It would be an enormous chore, due to the amount of their mail. Thus we deal here with "allegations"—the proofs remain to be brought about later. Would we have the time and take the trouble? The busy parish is more pre-occupied with prayer, with life and the fruits than the verification. We are dealing with testimonies given in good faith, like those we find in the Bible and in centuries past. They indicate presumably that the supernatural of Scottsdale is not only spiritual or interior. There are astonishing consequences (such as the Latin word *miraculum*) and recognized as such by many doctors—those who have benefited have no doubt.

If the official commission reopens its investigations, it would be well to consider these healings and others, because there is an extraordinary and exceptional action of God in this place. In the Church as well as in the Bible, everything starts with the spontaneous discernment of the faithful *(sensus fidelium)*. In the time of Jesus Christ and the first centuries, they would rely on this *vox populi*.

For apparitions and healings (like the "renowned sanctity" which is the starting point for canonization), the sense of the faithful has its value and possesses the *conditio possidentis*. From these benefits, the technical and spiritual verifications of the authority must act.

CHAPTER 10

Messages

We have already presented the initial stages and the general sense of the message in the second chapter.

Should we present here a synthesis or overview? It is premature in this respect, because this message continues. It is an unfinished symphony. Let us be careful not to end it prematurely.

On the other hand, this message defies the synthesis, because it is not a constructed doctrine, not even one to construct. It is a living pedagogy which speaks to our heart, guides a group, a parish, and others through them. Its aim is to change hearts and should be read. But it should also be part of the fruits instead of just reading it on paper.

Finally, the deeds and the behavior of the visionaries, of the prayer groups, and of the parish are part of the message. The Word of God is not just reduced to words. It is filtered through life and the events in the history of salvation—in the Church of today like in the Bible. I had called attention to this rule of interpretation from my very first book on Lourdes *(Sense of Lourdes)* in 1954: "Apparitions are God's language, which speaks within its people and in the history. This history is part of the message," I said, "and should be acknowledged however often we forget."

In this perspective, the first word of the message from Lourdes is "poverty." This word was not uttered by Our Blessed Mother, but it was a state of being, the very choice of Bernadette, who was a member of the poorest family in the village. During the famine of 1856, the police had come to arrest her father, because of the simple fact that "the state of his misery presumed him guilty of theft." Those whom the police had come to take away, to be charged and sent to prison, Our Blessed Mother had chosen. Bernadette was conscious of that fact. Many witnesses of the apparitions perceived this, as did the bishop himself in his judgment where he recognized the apparitions. It is important to bring to light this integral and misunderstood part of the message of Lourdes. The problem is the same in Scottsdale.

Examining the messages will not lead us to a synthesis strictly speaking, like in Lourdes or Medjugorje, because the events and the messages here have a different character. It is less synthetic, nearer to life itself, given occasionally to the thread of life. And this is what has spoken to the hearts of the people of God across the country.

Here like anywhere else, and more so than most, an intellectual synthesis of the message will always be deceiving if we are not able to read it in the very life of the people that it vivifies. Having said this, we can now try to extract its meaning.

The Names of the Visionaries

In the Bible, many persons (from Abraham to Mary, then Simon to Saul, becoming Peter and Paul), received a new name from God which explained their mission or vocation. In Scottsdale, everyone of the group received such a name or symbol.

In the overall, the ten express synthetically a program and a message. Moreover:

"These names are all virtues from the heart of Jesus," summarized Fr. Spaulding.

It is significant that three visionaries have received the name of the three theological virtues, those which allow us to reach God Himself—FAITH, HOPE, CHARITY. These three words are repeated often in the messages (Vol. I, pages 19, 22, 23, 28, 42, 57, 59, 78, 89; Vol. II, pages 42, etc.). This centering on the theological virtues, those that refer us to God, is very meaningful.

—FAITH allows us to reach the hidden God Who has revealed

Himself to us in His **truth** (the symbolic name given to Fr. Spaulding).

—HOPE allows us to reach God by desire and at the same time by (His) merciful power: kindness, generosity. Hope transfigures the desire and the will to attain Him.

—CHARITY allows us to reach Him in His goodness, by communion. God is Love and all the action of God is love: both creation and salvation. But in our human language the word "love" is ambiguous. "I love you" can mean:

—I love you for myself. That is eros, desire, egoism, or

—I love you for yourself. That is agape, gift, generosity.

The love of God (Agape) is truly a gift. He creates all the goodness of His creatures. God does not destroy the natural eros, but He completes and transfigures it by His Agape. This conversion of selfish love into divine love is the act of forgetting ourselves for the other. Thus we find in Divine Agape the hundredfold return promised by Christ. This is the love God invites us to indirectly by sacrifice: *Anyone who finds his life will lose it; anyone who loses his life for my sake will find it,* as seen throughout Matthew's gospel (*Matt.* 10:39, 16:25; *Mark* 8:38; *Luke* 9:24; 17:33).

This is the mysterious law of our destiny—the very same life of Christ. His human life illustrates the greatest proof of love: *No one can have greater love than to lay down his life for his friends (John* 15:13). God-made-man lived a painful journey for the salvation of mankind. In short, Agape transfigures the *desire* via a *gift*, without which there is no true love.

The other names given by Our Lady are in total harmony with this fundamental orientation:

—TRUTH, the very purpose of our faith. God is TRUTH, the measure and source of all truths.

—JOY, is the happiness of love, because there is no happiness without love, and such is Divine Happiness. The messages of Jesus begin with the Beatitudes: "HAPPY," He repeats before each, manifesting the austerity of our journey through poverty, tears and persecution (*Matt.* 5:3-11); (*Luke* 6:20-22).

Three other names signify asceticism, calling to mind
sequela Christi: by the cross, toward the Resurrection, but
these are also virtues that the Holy Spirit gives to accomplish
this trial.
—HUMILITY: "I am Who am, you are who is not," said God
to Saint Catherine of Sienna. Christians cannot accomplish
great things except through the truth of His humility; because
humility is but truth, acknowledging that we owe all to our
Creator: our being, our life, and our holiness. It is by humility
that we discover hope and thus await for everything from God,
our transcending Creator.

Humility is not annihilating, but on the contrary, it is a tonic
attitude because humility connects us to HOPE and the power
of God (it gives us courage to cope). Mary Cook, who
has received this name, understands this well.
—STRENGTH and COURAGE are the seventh and eighth
names given to the group of ten, according to the order
in which we list them. We refer to strength as the strength
of God: the gift that the Holy Spirit gives to the weak of
this world to triumph.

Mercy

But the main point of the message in Scottsdale, which
became the title of the book of the messages, is **MERCY**. This
word is a focal point of the gospel. It signifies kindness,
benevolence, thanksgiving, compassion, gentleness. Mercy, a
favorable reception to someone who is in a difficult situation—
even to our enemies. David showed mercy for Saul who was
fighting him. He spared him when he had him at his mercy.

This word has profound biblical roots. In Hebrew, it is *hèsed*,
which means fidelity of God and His benevolence toward sinners and the unfortunates; and also *hén*, which expresses an
inclination of the heart toward others. The Greek word is *eleos*,
which we find in the *Kyrie eleison:* "Lord, have mercy." The
corresponding Latin word, *misericordia* is formed on the basis
of the word heart *(cor, cordis)*. It signifies open attitude, generous, cordial toward the unfortunate *(miseri)*. It implies "compassion" (the symbolic name given to Jimmy).

There is a closer relationship to the Hebrew word: *rahamin* (Greek: *splagkna*) in regard to this attitude of the entrails of mercy *(misericordia)*. The Bible characterizes God by this visceral word: referring to the maternal breast, and also to the the paternal entrails. Here lies the physical expression of love, creator of life. This is not a trivial word. Paternity and maternity awakens in the parents, deep within the depth of their entrails, treasures of generosity, of gifts, of tenderness, of forgetting of one's self, such as they never thought possible. We find this image in the paternal instinct in animals. According to mythology, the pelican nourished his starving young with his own entrails. Such is God's love. Jesus nourishes us with His body. He created us in His image to imitate and share this love.

Mercy translates God's very own attitude: He asks us to forgive the offenses of our enemies and even to love our enemies. And there resides the specificity of the Christian message, going beyond the ancient law.

Semiotics Diagram

In order to accede to the synthesis of the message, I have attempted to make the semiotics square, according to the structure which manifests 4 aspects of the same contrast: 2 contrary, which opposes itself horizontally, and their contradictories which are excluded diagonally. The analysis has brought me to this following square:

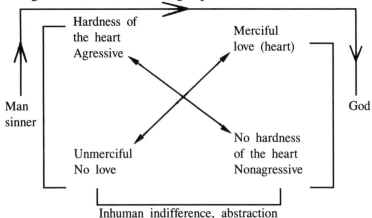

Explanation:

Man-Sinner characterizes himself by being hard—without mercy (the accolade on the left). God, by Mercy without hardness of the heart, forms the accolade on the right.

The journey (trajectory), as proposed by the message, leads from this hardness to Mercy by which we reach God, according to the petitions to the Father: *Forgive us our trespasses as we forgive those who trespass against us.*

As far as the accolade at the bottom, those who have neither mercy nor hardness of the heart, it is the inhuman indifference, the abstraction without aggressiveness, which we encounter here also on earth and which could have frightening side effects.

This analysis clarifies the outstanding or central point. It would not pretend to be exhaustive. It is but the first semiotics' unravelling of the concept.

Intuitive Synthesis of the Message

It is not easy then to propose an organic synthesis of the message of Scottsdale. Those who succeed better are those who live the message interiorly, because it is the seed of life and not a superstructural teaching.

"Just, simple and penetrating," would seem to me the synthesis of Fr. Robert Wells after two trips to Scottsdale. He found an intimate experience of the messages. Here is the essential of Fr. Well's analysis: "To capture in a few words, the heart of the message is difficult," he starts, but ends happily in saying:

"We hasten to take seriously the call of Baptism to holiness. It calls for allowing God to become the center of our lives by a life of prayer and in God's loving service and that of our neighbors. It is a call to obedience, faith, in union with the teachings of the Church, under the actual leadership of Pope John Paul II. We have to allow Jesus to restore love, compassion, Mercy, dignity, respect and honesty for the human race. It is a loving and urgent appeal to our hearts, for our hearts.

"Briefly, it is the Gospel's appeal for us to confide in the merciful love of God, Our Father, as it was revealed by His son Jesus Christ, Our Savior, by the action of the Holy Spirit ...in my own heart and in the heart of those whom I met in Scottsdale. To abandon one's self totally to God, that is our challenge, and a daily struggle in all our lives, according to the call to follow the road to holiness, accompanied by the painful awareness of our sinfulness. Saint Maria Goretti is not Utopia, but it is a place where the Mercy of God was revealed to these children...

"Finally, it is a spirit full of urgent hope which permeates the unfolding events in Scottsdale. The message reminds us that we are living in a time of grace, in a time of Divine Mercy."

Father Jack Spaulding, interrogated on the overall view (ensemble) of the messages, said in a convergent manner:

> "All these messages and lessons encourage us to keep God in the center of our hearts. These are words of love and concern, of challenge and mercy, an invitation to hope."

This intuitive expression ties in very well with the analysis that we have presented starting with the names (symbols) given to the ten. It is an invitation to theocentricism. It is an attitude centered on God Himself by the theological virtues: (Father Jack names explicitly **hope** and **love**), and more precisely an obligation, a concern, this "Divine Mercy" which is the specific center of the message.

"It is simply an actualization of the Gospel," pursues Fr. Jack, "an invitation to Salvation in passing through death to eternal life, by an authentic conversion of the heart."

The word conversion is also central in the message and in the fruits, like in Lourdes and in Medjugorje. All is centered on conversion, underlines Fr. Spaulding. The message actualizes then the first pages in the Gospel: the preaching of John the Baptist, and the preliminary invitation of Jesus in *Mark* 1:15: *The Kingdom of God is at hand. Reform your lives and believe in the gospel.''* In other words, convert.

Progression

It is more difficult to discern the progression and stages in the messages. Volume 1 of *I Am Your Jesus Of Mercy* stresses the formation of the theological virtues and of the complimentary virtues of Sincerity (pg. 15), Simplicity (pg. 21, Humility (pg. 64), Respect (pg. 31), Gratitude (pg. 32), Obedience (pg. 37), Pardon (pg. 82, etc.) and the struggle against vices which dwell in our civilization, Envy (pg. 51), Selfishness (pg. 30), Pride (pg. 65), Vanity (pg. 93, etc.). There is also suggestion of the Trinity (pg. 50), of the Kingdom (pg. 88), of the Presence of God (pgs. 38, 54), of the Passion (pgs. 9, 47), of Fasting (pg. 25) and of Prayer of the heart (pg. 56).

In Volume II, there is suggestion on Sainthood (pg. 26), but also on Suffering (pgs. 16, 21), Weariness (pg. 15), Growth (pg. 52), and Spiritual healing (pg. 6). There also appears *sequela Christi* (Discipleship, pg. 65).

This theme appears in Volume III, (pg. 7 line 3), as well as the Reign of God (pg. 24), Illumination (pg. 25), Church (pg. 29) and Peace (pg. 32), but also Difficulties (pg. 4) and Redemptive suffering (pg. 14).

Along the pedagogical avenues, Our Lady talks first (on July 14, 1988), in order to prepare for the messages of Jesus (September), which refer to the Holy Spirit and to the Trinity (pgs. 31-50).

This pedagogy teaches us to live *love*, cultivated less by the theological faculties then by the groups' concern for the formation of faith and prayer in a humble setting. From there we receive the counsels, by way of a psychological forewarning on the virtues and the vices (especially in the first volume). We risk removing the freshness from the message in the process of too much analysis, or in enumerating too many terms. They often come in a rhythm, in line with the unforseeable realities of our own lives.

"The important thing," Bill Reck told me, "is that we see a growth in people's lives in response to the messages in *I Am Your Jesus Of Mercy*. From our point of view, this message is not measured according to theological barometers, but by the addressee. The many letters that we receive from the readers of the messages are very positive, very glowing."

According to Father Jack Spaulding and many others in the group, Our Lady has come to America to fight the devil on his own turf, where he has lain seige by priority, considering the immense power of this country, the only remaining "Big" after the destabilization of Russia. The nine visionaries' mission is to live and diffuse a model that ordinary people themselves can imitate. They give proof that all can convert. And this will be able to spread.

CHAPTER 11

The Meaning and the Future

And now, where will Scottsdale go? What sense, and in
what direction should be its standard?

Signification

If the spiritual movement of Scottsdale has seemed important enough to merit writing a book about it, it is because
of the awakening of the Christians within a united parish that
is significant for the life of the Church.

Since the 1970's, a movement of prayer was born within
the Church. It began in mid 1968, during the crossing of
the desert which followed Vatican II. It was a profound start,
a return to the essential, to the source, because prayer is
respiration itself of the Christian soul. It is not a monologue
but a communication. We address ourselves to God and we,
in return, receive His light, inspirations and motions, which
improve, transform and deify our lives.

A rupture in communication is harmful in all domestic
relationships. It is true in a family, between husband and
wife, parents and children, between friends. More so with
God. And still man is inclined to build Berlin walls practically everywhere.

The movement of Scottsdale is founded on prayer. Such was
the first objective of St. Maria Goretti Parish from the outset.
It centered on the Eucharist. From this well-oriented faith
were born three prayer groups.

—The Thursday night "Our Lady's Prayer Group" (Mass as
the focal point);

—Friday for young adults, those 20 to 35;
—Monday for the teens.

And these groups have not ceased to grow. The Thursday group sometimes numbers as many as 500 persons. This rediscovery of living prayer has progressively radiated all over the United States.

In our materialistic world where God is marginal, even excluded, these clear and sensitive communications confirm to all that God is there; He is alive, He is intimate. Prayer has developed an habitual union with God for many, and as usual, charisms followed. This started particular forms of communication, such as locutions or apparitions and then others. The exercising of the charisms fortifies the health of the soul, just as exercising fortifies the health of the body.

Certainly, ordinary prayer is important to faith, fortified according to the words of Christ: *Happy are those who have not seen but have believed.* Apparitions, locutions and other sensitive signs have helped those whose faith was being asphyxiated and have rediscovered vitality and happiness. God has provided like a good Father. Mary has cooperated like a good Mother. This overture to the Holy Spirit has aroused benevolent charisms: First of all healings. They always appear there where the Church is alive. Thus, it is also an overture to the sick and more widely to the poor. It is in this sense that Wendy's vocation is outlined.

This overture to God also stirs asceticism, notably fasting, sacrifice, a profound union with the Passion of Our Lord (including stigmata). The charism of "victim soul" (frightening no doubt but which was also present in Our Lord—the Sacrificed Lamb, Our Blessed Mother in her compassion, and the martyred apostles) always had its place in the Body of Christ throughout the centuries, under many forms. And, it is not absent from the group of these visionaries. It is the underlying incentive of Redemption in progress. Francis of Assisi succeeded in making it understood that it goes hand in hand with joy. Susan Evans lives this trial.

In Scottsdale, this awakening of the charisms developed without disturbing the unity of the parish. Charisms do not upset ordinary faith, they nourish. They have remained sufficiently discreet in order to help those who are most in need and offend no one. They have been an attraction and not an obstacle. It is important that they keep this status. We will come back to this later.

This radiance is widespread as indicated by the great demand for the message books, best-sellers in the religious market. Evidently their success is a response to a need, at a time when so many Christians, who are lethargic and underfed, become prey to sects. The radiance of the messages is good news.

That this Christian experience would have succeeded is comforting after a sad example in Lubbock, Texas, equally a by-product of Medjugorje, and analogous circumstances to Scottsdale. But in Lubbock the movement was broken by a unilateral repression. At the end of a quick investigation, a competent Commission had concluded, like in Scottsdale, not to withhold proof that there could be miracles. And this was formulated in the habitual terms (however ambiguous) used in this matter: "it is not supernatural."

The worthy pastor was silenced in order to put an end to this nonsupernatural. . .which had multiplied prayer, confession, conversions and generosity in the parish. The negative decision could have been reached because a too quick development of the charisms, being insufficiently discreet, had created a division in the parish. But many of the experts who had been called to this fast-moving investigation have regretted this negative interpretation, and at least one of them has made it known to a competent authority.

Evolution of the Visionaries

Those among the first six, then the nine, who have not yet received any particular charisms (locutions, apparitions), are called to have some, according to Gianna's premonitions. Is this what is happening? Prophets are not infallible. But this prediction stimulates from the interior, a momentum, a hope, a source of fundamental progression which alone is important. Suspense dwells.

Perhaps here is where we should state precisely (in a way that is not indiscreet) where the nine are and where they are going, as of my second trip to Scottsdale in May of 1992.

1. Susan

Susan Evans, afflicted with poor health and partial deafness, is following a fruitful but suffering path. On August 15, 1991, she received this request from Our Lord:
—*Will you still suffer for Me?*
She reported this modestly, like a willing person would do. It is quite apparent that Susan's sufferings play a major role in these events. Her health handicaps her more and more and she is not working. She lives modestly on Social Security and has given away her possessions according to Christ's desires. She has abandoned herself to Him totally. What impressed me most was her luminous smile in spite of her burden. At times her suffering is more profound and she asks Our Lord: "For how many more sinners?" But He does not answer.

"We do not get used to suffering," I told her.

"Yes, but grace gives us even the desire to suffer if it is for the salvation of sinners and for Our Lord," she replied.

In Medjugorje, Vicka suffered similarly and has stated: "Suffering is to remain silent. But when it becomes unbearable, grace is strong enough to find a smile." Susan is a subterranean strength for this parish.

When Vassula Ryden (who knows what it is to share Our Lord's Passion) was passing through Phoenix in April of 1992, she visited Scottsdale. She met and understood Susan. It was especially Susan whom she talked to me about.

2. Gianna

Gianna experiences triple trials.
—Charisms lead her in a breathtaking cadence, rhythm. The very richness of her gifts and blessings (graces) are difficult

to assume. She is pushed to human limits, which could cause her reticence and distrusts.

—She is going through a profound spiritual night, illuminated only by the rare apparitions of Our Lady.

—To this are added rejection, separation from close friends, including her husband (her marriage was annulled in February 1992) and internal suffering.

In August 1991, she received an eighth secret, not only from Our Lord, but from Our Lady. Some of the previous seven have materialized already. She is not aware if they coincide with those from Medjugorje. She holds the same commitment of secrecy.

She and Annie Ross participated at the Anaheim, California Charismatic Convention, August 31 to September 1. During the major prayer service, August 31, there were healings. A man got out of his wheelchair and walked. Many were slain in the Spirit. This phenomena, often misunderstood, is the grace of a total relaxation of the body, of the psychic and of the spirit. The physical relaxation provokes falling but those who fall do not get hurt. They get up renewed, purified and liberated from tensions and interior temptations.

The same thing happened on Sunday, September 1, when Father Robert Faricy, professor of spirituality at the Gregorian University of Rome, prayed over people along with Gianna. Gianna wrote to me that she was worried to see so many fall because mimicry can amplify such phenomena. Was this a response to my letter to her saying?: "Healings bring more than resting in the Spirit, and the spiritual night that you are experiencing faithfully is more important than the healings themselves."

At the end of this Convention, Father Faricy and Gianna recited the Rosary, and Gianna states she had an apparition. Many claimed to have seen a bright light when Our Blessed Mother came, or during her presence.

Gianna went to Rome from September 28 to October 17, 1991, to relay a message discreetly to the Pope. During her trip, she states she had her third apparition of Jesus. And it was the next day that she met Pope John Paul II, after Mass. The comprehension was immediate and brief, at the same time discreet. Gianna does not know in what language they spoke, but they understood each other.

Another purpose of this trip was to find her calling. She had considered Oasis of Peace, a prosperous Medjugorje community near Rome. But all things considered, she and Fr. Gianni Sgreva, decided her mission lies elsewhere, perhaps as a lay person but in the U.S.A. Things are getting clearer and clearer for her.

Upon her return, she found herself swamped with projects. She wisely chose one that she already had started to develop with others, according to her competence in the medical and pharmaceutical fields. In the U.S.A., the limitations of Social Security create serious problems for the sick, often incapable of seeking necessary care because of lack of funds. She has founded, with others, project MOM *(Mission of Mercy)*, which will provide free basic medical care by mobile unit to the homeless, poor, and transients. She was guided toward the priority of the poor, notably concerning health: specifically for the aged.

"They need love and attention. They would like to have respect and dignity. I have a great love for them," she wrote.

Wasn't this the same concern of Our Lord who performed miracles? Gianna is often asked to pray for healing but she realizes that it is not a panacea, a cure-all. She mobilizes human means for the priority of the poor, recommended in the Gospel and by John Paul II. Her talent does not lie in money-making, thus the slow process of carrying out her project.

She returned from Rome and Assisi, on October 22, 1991. She drew important spiritual conclusions of her trip, and her pilgrimage to Assisi, concerning her personal life, and also the desires and plans of Our Lord, Himself. Herewith she provides a resume:

1. Jesus loves the souls who adore Him in a simple, pure way WITHOUT looking for consolation.
2. Do not hope in the message, hope in the Lord.
3. It is not what you do that gives you peace: peace is a gift. Peace and happiness are not the result of what kind of work you accomplish.
4. You cannot find peace, it is peace that finds you.
5. It is our very own existence that proclaims the goodness of God...It is easy to praise Him sincerely, with thanksgiving, even in our struggles, the most difficult ones, if we understand His love and His mercy (Mercy...in forgiving ourselves). In Assisi, Our Lord talked to me a lot at the Carceri. He said that on our journey with God, we all have to do it alone. The road is narrow. He alone can guide us safely, because He made this journey before we did. We are a people of imperfections, and we can become perfect only through Him. We take halting steps like a lame person, but each step is beautiful and it has its own impact. He is the one who makes straight our walk.

On November 17, 1991, she went to pray in Kansas City, where 900 persons were waiting for her. After adoration of the Blessed Sacrament, she prayed for all of them. There evidently were conversions and healings (interior and physical, notably a nun with sight problems). But Gianna refused to stay and chat with the people. She had come only to pray.

Since May 1990, she is in a severe spiritual night. Moreover, she carries, in the communion of the saints, the burden of sinners, as did Our Lord carrying His cross: an invisible cross which does not alter her drive, or her smile.

Note:

In May of 1992 Channel 3 of Phoenix (ABC Network) requested permission to run a news series on the events at St. Maria Goretti. Included was to be a film sequence of Gianna's ecstasy in her home. Bishop O'Brien was consulted and gave his benevolent permission. I was present in the room-chapel where Gianna has her daily ecstasy. The filmed sequence took place on May 6th, from 8 to 8:06 p.m. during the Rosary led by Father Jack in front of the statue of Our Lady of Fatima which was flanked by two candles. It was a fervent and simple ceremony. During the apparition, Gianna did not see the surroundings or the statue but only the luminous appearance of the Mother of God.

After the Rosary, Fr. Jack, Mary Cook, Steve Nelson and myself were interviewed concerning the ecstasy and its meaning. The report was to be initially shown on TV on May 17th and I was a witness to the transparent presence of Our Lady in our material world.

3. Mary

Mary Cook had interior visions. They had stopped in October 1990. Her mission is to pray for unborn babies. In the fall of 1991, Mary again started receiving messages at the prayer group meeting on Fridays. The locutions come from both Our Lord and Our Lady. In keeping with her vocation of working with children, Mary has recently been added to the staff of St. Maria Goretti. This year she will initiate a pre-school program teaching small children of the parish. It is in keeping with Mary's growth. She, like Wendy, exhibits a new and profound spiritual maturity.

4. Steve

Steve Nelson continues his life of work and prayer and participates in the Thursday night prayer group. He has sacrificed his dream of roping and has relinquished sports in favor of an austere prayer life. His radiant joy, always apparent, comes from deep within. He continues to discern his future and waits patiently for the Lord. This patience has recently provided definite fruits. Steve was anxious and troubled regarding the responsibility of marriage and children. In the spring of 1992, he found great peace in his decision to marry and was busy making plans for his marriage to Susan Raheb on June 20, 1992.

5. Wendy

Wendy Nelson is clearly and enthusiastically pursuing a career of serving the poor and she continues her studies in sociology. She is blessed with apparitions of Our Lady (which seem to come out of the statue). Her path resembles that of her brother. Her enthusiasm is pure and sound, with an active abandonment to Our Lord. Wendy appears to be growing in self-assurance, both in her personal goals and in her role of the events at St. Maria Goretti. She appears happy and content with her current status and her goals.

6. Jimmy

I had the pleasure to meet with Jimmy in May of 1992. He is very likeable, patient and searching for his path. It is a difficult road. He will complete his college studies this year, specializing in communications, and is very stimulated toward this field. His talents of animation and being a guitarist have been of great service to the young people of the parish. He would like to continue in this vein with employment in the music ministry at the parish and arranging projects for TV filming.

In addition to his periodical contacts with Fr. Jack, Jimmy has recourse to Fr. Alberto Ruiz, a Claretian, who is in charge of the Cursillo Movement in the Phoenix Diocese, and who acts as his spiritual director. Our Lord and Our Lady manifest themselves to him somewhat like the intimate experience of the disciple from Emmaus, a burning heart. But now it appears to be in a new stage: the spiritual night. He is blessed with a real spiritual yearning. In the interim, Jimmy continues his studies with a strong desire to manifest what he is experiencing to the youth, in God's behalf.

7. Stefanie

Stefanie Staab, who had previously abandoned her prestigious position in computers and economics because of health problems, resumed her career in 1991. Jesus has explained to her the meaning of humility through this trial.

In 1990 she experienced spiritual difficulties and was for a time without any messages.

In August 1991 (her sufferings were more spiritual than physical), Father Faricy counseled her about her going through the "Dark Night," and that it was a time of maturing. Thus she has progressed in prayer and mercy. Those around her can attest to this.

She has difficulties with the presence of the devil, but Our Lord has permitted this to happen to show His complete power over Satan.

She does not have apparitions, but says that on September 13, 1990, she received a promise that ulteriorly she would— to help her in time of stress and need, and to help her in her role of emissary for the parish community. She still continues to receive messages through locutions.

8. James Pauley

I was not expecting too much from this young man of 22 years, but I was deeply impressed with his evident and profound spiritual growth. He is completely absorbed in his full-time position in the parish in the formation of teenagers. He moulds them in their prayer and does it with great joy because he himself has become a man of prayer. He does more than teach, he radiates and shares with these young people who are preparing for Confirmation (fixed at age 16 in the diocese). He has modesty, assuredness and authority which I found striking and which radiates from deep within, much like with Mary and Wendy.

Even with his tight schedule he continues to pursue his studies at a local college and even relaxes on weekends by playing basketball. He is waiting to receive the particular graces of locutions or apparitions (he does not know which)—they were not promised to him.

9. Annie Ross (Fitch)

On August 31, 1991, a month after my first interview with her, Annie Ross attended the Charismatic Convention in Anaheim, California, with Gianna. She says Our Lord had invited her to come but she decided to go only at the last minute due to a lack of funds.

That Sunday, she and Gianna prayed over the crowd. There were many people who were slain in the spirit and apparently healings occurred. During the evening of the same Sunday, Annie had planned to have dinner with Father Robert DeGrandis but she was not feeling well and decided not to eat. She stated that during the evening Jesus appeared to her and asked her if she would suffer for humanity. She suffered for 45 minutes and additionally then experienced the pain of the "crown of thorns."

Following this, Annie said she had a vision of a host, then a white cross. Jesus came out of the cross and told her that she suffered His cross, bore His wounds. She says Jesus told her "We are One. Human love cannot interfere with this."

This could have seemed to signify that her marriage, originally planned for December 21, 1991, would be subject to change. We will see later its interpretation in a more exclusive sense.

Father DeGrandis, from the state of Louisiana and friend of Father Spaulding, was near her throughout until the morning. During that night, Annie says she saw devils, who wanted to attack her. Father DeGrandis said prayers of exorcism. Eric, her fiance, was there also, and prayed for her as well.

On September 12, 1991, she says that she received a new message from Our Lady:

My child, do not be afraid, I will not appear to you as before, you will not see me with human eyes but with the eyes of your soul. I will appear to you on your birthday, like I had promised and in time of great difficulty, the rest of your life according to my Son's will. Be at peace. Have confidence in Him.

My dear child, do not be afraid, I will never abandon you. You are mine. When we will talk, you will see clearly with the eyes of your soul. (. . .)

"And she left. Since this experience, I have talked often with Our Lady. Henceforth, I ask Her advice on what to do, whatever it is. I see Her (spiritually) in a way as loving and as magnificent as always. She is the most lovable of all, beyond any human comprehension. She is brilliant with light owing to her purity and her perfection.

"I also talk with Our Lord daily. He directs me according to His will. We pray together sometimes.

"I have now closed my flower shop. I have confidence in Our Lord, because He has promised to take care of us. . . He always does what He promises.

"Our Lord has appeared to me—I see Him with the eyes of my soul. I see Him in all His majesty and splendor, in color and in a precise manner. (. . .) My role entails many facets. My first role is to be an example of humility for the world. This is not a small task for me, who am so arrogant, prideful in my personality. *Humility* is the symbol which was given to me by Our Lady and Our Lord. Our Lady explained to me that humility is the willingness to serve God with all my heart, all my spirit and all my body and all my soul, without any reservation or hesitation. . . It is the desire to serve others at all times, for the love of God.

"The second point is to pray for the salvation of mankind and for the souls in Purgatory, to suffer in union with Our Lord and to pray with others for spiritual and physical healing.

"The third point would be to pray for priests and the religious, for our Holy Father, Pope John Paul II, seminarians and novitiates and the increase of vocations."

During autumn 1991, Annie gave her life to Our Lord. She was made aware of great difficulties. She met Father Faricy on September 15 and Father DeGrandis on the 27th, whom she chose for her spiritual director. She stated that on October 17, the suffering of the Cross intensified. Annie's response was total acceptance and confidence.

This re-oriented profoundly her whole being, barely one month before her marriage, originally planned for December 21, 1991. She was now contemplating the religious life. She decided to postpone the marriage. It was a tragic decision for her fiance, Eric, who had accepted to follow her to the end of this exacting path, not knowing that it would lead to separation from her.

After many long weeks she received evidence from Our Lady that the marriage was holy and compatible with the divine union to Christ. Their break-up was perhaps but a trial. Everything worked out and the marriage was celebrated on February 17, 1992. Annie is now a parishioner in another parish since the marriage and has become more involved with her spiritual director in the charismatic renewal.

We have not finished with surprises from Scottsdale. God's ways are not so linear and foreseeable as man's ways.

If I have dedicated more time to two visionaries, Gianna and Annie, it is not that I place more importance on them but because they live a significant itinerary and thanks to their confidence and their requests for counseling, I had the opportunity to follow them more closely than the others. The length of their write-up does not indicate a judgment of value.

Like in Medjugorje, the visionaries or locutionists are very different from one another. Their itineraries are very diversified. The devil takes this opportunity to try to cause division among them or with their pastor, who is overworked with so many imperative tasks. To this point, they seem to have been able to rise above these temptations.

10. Father Jack

Father Jack Spaulding continues to guide this movement that is exacting as well as difficult to manage. Not only does everything go fast—the Holy Spirit initiatives, those of the visionaries—but he also has to maintain the equilibrium and the unity between the prudent requests of the bishop and the dynamic enthusiasm of the visionaries. There is need to curtail any tension between the parishioners' openness to the new graces (blessings), and those who are bound to former and traditional forms of the parish, and finally, between the parishioners and the flood of pilgrims.

Some find him difficult. This would not be part of his personality by personal choice. It is the result of multiple and extreme tensions, in many respects, insurmountable. He is a man of worth: receptive, generous, hospitable. He was chosen to guide this work. He needs help for this great task, which is beyond human forces.

The Risks

Like all life that is expanding, growing, it is subject to risks.

1. There are always inherent tensions in all life, and also in all dynamic communities. It has been there since the beginning of the Church.

2. There is the spiritual struggle, which is law itself of all authentic supernatural life: whether it be for the person or the community. When a group leaves the beaten path and disengages itself from mediocrity, the devil multiplies the pitfalls against those who threaten his reign. Jesus was not exempt from this battle: Temptations in the desert, His violent death where He suffered the trial of dereliction (*Mark* 15:34). Histories of the saints do not fail to witness this in various degrees throughout the centuries. The devil has the art not only to create obstacles and discouragement, but to arouse imaginative outbursts, both pious and ecstatic, which visionaries could take as divine motions. The visionaries of Scottsdale have suffered temptations of this type and were able to overcome them with discernment.

3. We must also avoid division that the presence of a fervent group risks creating in the masses (faithful). The exigency of perfection of some, their zeal, even their appearance of a superiority complex, can soon provoke negative reactions, with division and fighting.

4. We must also outwit the tensions, which never failed to appear in the course of the centuries, between the charisms and the authority. Fr. Karl Rahner analyzed this

phenomenon very well. He felt that when visionaries and prophets emerge, Christians too often find God in them instead of finding Him in the ministry. Authority is overshadowed. In the course of the centuries, as a result of these mechanisms of rejection, the repressions extinguished the Spirit and disintegrated fervent communities. But in Scottsdale, the parish always exercised modesty.

5. But obedience is not without a matter of conscience when it appears to stifle the Spirit, Christian certitude, or to limit expansion. Conciliation is often difficult, even agonizing. But the Scottsdale group defended itself very well against this. Hopefully this problem will not grow with the constant development of the charisms.

The Future

What then is the future of this movement of grace?

Personally, I hesitate to predict an international future for Scottsdale—to make it another "Lourdes" as one would say, or another "Fatima." There are many reasons. It is not necessary that an apparition make an entire population run to a site, thus making it a tourist attraction. Besides, being a celebrity is a heavy and dangerous burden. Power corrupts, and glory also, helped by temptation. At any rate, the diffusion of the charisms hoped for by John XXIII in Vatican II are called most often to a modest career. Isn't that the discretion Bishop O'Brien had encouraged for Scottsdale, which has succeeded thus far?

The *"I Am Your Jesus of Mercy"* books have helped spread the radiance of this parish throughout America. One of the visionaries wrote to me on October 28, 1991:

> "Our Lady is said to have come here because she wishes to protect America. Jesus allowed her to come here. She asks that our country use its immense power for the glory of God. In fact, she invites us to live in love, mercy, compassion, respect, dignity and honesty."

I would be more inclined toward this national vocation, notably to vivify prayer in American parishes. But, in Scottsdale (as in San Nicolas), those who live the events see a greater scope. Already, they say the influx of visitors reflects an international radiance since the Spanish translation of the messages books has been completed. Finally, it seems to be in accordance with Our Lady's wishes and as per certain messages dictate.

What will happen in the case of Scottsdale? Will it exceed the limits of the English speaking world and that of the Hispanic people in regard to San Nicolas? The answer is beyond the critical discernment of an expert. It all depends on the Holy Spirit and human freedom. Time (future) will tell.

CHAPTER 12

Personal and Ecclesiastical
Dimension of Scottsdale

Mystical Dimension

In Scottsdale, a city typical of any other, in the parish of St. Maria Goretti, typical of many others, the Holy Spirit has poured out one of the numerous gifts which give new life to the Church as we prepare for the start of the third millenium: *that they might have life and have it to the fullest* (*John* 10:10). It was a fundamental wish of Christ.

Our Lord comes, preceded and prepared by His Mother, like 2000 years ago. The time is near. He talks, He questions, interpellates, to make Himself understood above the technical and mediatic hubbub with which our ears have been bombarded.

It calls to mind His fundamental existence under the sign of Incarnation. It is God transcendant. He presents Himself for adoration, and that is the very life of this parish, where adoration is available in a special chapel (Tabernacle) for this fundamental act. He is all, and does not demand less than all. This may seem frightening, but not in Scottsdale. The visionaries and others have confidence in Him, and they well understand that if God asks for all, it is that He wants to give us infinitely all: Himself, His absolute love, the only One capable of fulfilling all our desires.

The transcendant God does not present Himself as distant and frightening. He is imminent and near. He does not crush

131

their freedom, but invites them to love. He comes simply and humanly under the sign of Mercy. He is God in the Gospel, come to call not the righteous but the sinners, and there is more joy when one sinner repents than with 99 just people who do not need repentence. But that is not all. He is not only the transcendent God, imminent, infinite and near. He is the One Who manifests His infinite love and His mercy by giving love until death, through abundance of suffering. He has asked many to share in His Passion, by trials of health or even by stigmatas, to finish what is lacking in the sufferings of Christ for the sake of His body, the Church (*Col.* 1:24).

"Life in abundance" generously given by Christ, passes through His Cross and sacrifices. The visionaries and the others commit themselves, without dispute or wincing, simply, freely, generously, in abandonment to love itself, which gives worth to the Cross, its fruits and its future. The Cross is where Christ gave His Spirit, and from where gushed forth a living source of water and blood pouring from the pierced side of Jesus.

This Divine Source has already manifested Its strength and Its expansiveness. It vivified, nearer and nearer, the nine young people called to this mission: these "yuppies," now having become children (children of God and of Mary). These young people of this world maintain their places, at different cultural levels, without being part of this world because they are of God and for God, and thus, more useful to the world. They are, in the Mystical Body of Christ, worthy channels of the Divine Source. In them flourishes a life of grace, fruitful in charisms, where the Holy Spirit edifies the community, that is to say, the Church. By their own strength and their talents they would not be able to accomplish any real renovation in the world without the strength of God, Who invigorates and allows them to bear fruit.

There is a profound solidarity between the parish and the visionaries at what is being accomplished elsewhere. They prefer a low profile without luster; but the Source from which they are channels, comes from God's abyss. This is how it works; this is how this grace has radiated on the parish, and from there, through the messages books, throughout the entire country.

Ecclesiastical Mission

It is not by chance that these graces have been eagerly accepted by a large number of people. They were in answer to a need born of spiritual hunger.

The spiritual movement of Scottsdale is very welcome, because it constitutes a remedy to the devitalizing abstractions which exhaust and sometimes cancerize· the Church.

1. Theological abstraction: born out of intellectualism, aggravated by an all negative criticism and by the closed ideologies of our time. The result is a weakening, even a vanishing of the personal, alive and existential relationship with God.
2. Administrative abstraction: because we allow organizations, officials, jurisdiction, finances, sociology to prevail over faith and life itself. This makes a number of institutions appear to be like empty shells: empty of God.

This double abstraction is aggravated by a polarization of man which makes him forget God: expansion of Anthropology without Theology. Mankind has been created by God, to return to God. We are not only animals blessed with an intelligence, but immortal animals, called to eternal life. In default of this evidence, revealed by God Himself, mankind becomes absurd. People have not meaning if they do not refer back to God.

All these deficiencies have opened the door to sects. They are strong by the very weaknesses of the Church. When sects cordially propose a living and demanding meeting with Jesus Christ, they find positive echos from spiritually under-fed Christians. This makes them successful, in spite of their deviations. Frightening is the crescendo of this phenomenon, cially in Latin America. It used to be the "Catholic Continent" par excellence, but its demographic expansion allowed Latin America to become the continent of sects.

In this conjecture, Scottsdale, and other places of prayer and of charisms, restored the presence of God, prayer, spiritual formation, authentic life of God and His radiance in the Church. It is the best prevention and the best antidote against the invasion of sects, before which our highest intellects lift their hands to Heaven without finding remedies or recipes. There is no recipe, save the authenticity of the divine life diffused and communicated. The radiance of Scottsdale holds to the fact that this parish proposes an accomplishment of the spiritual and divine dimension of man, by prayer, which is "the soul of all apostolate" as Dom Chautard said at the beginning of this century—too often forgotten today.

This world not only needs a supplement of the soul, but the soul is in need of a divine supplement which is essential to our being. This is what Scottsdale is witnessing.

We then are not just simple animals, reasonable and capriciously collated in the zoo of the cosmos among ordinary animals and pure spirits, like a paradoxal link in the chain of creation. We are not just an animal called to live in the instant, and then to disappear in euthanasia—according to Gide. Nor as theologian Pohier's preconceived idea in eliminating eternal life, are we just to cultivate the psychological happiness of the instant.

In this world of sin, where He came, where He died, where He resurrected, God always allows His source of life to flow, even though at times the channels of its diffusion may be obtuse and blocked. Our Lord does not remedy this lack of love and receptivity by a slap on the hands with His magic stick, but with love only. **He is Love,** owing to nothing else but to the love and to the freedom of mankind, whom He has created with love. This is what the example of the message of Scottsdale wants our deaf ears to understand.

The Supernatural and the Miraculous

The Source of the Problem

We probably are repeating this key-point, but worldwide the Commissions on ecclesiastical investigations of apparitions remain caught up in so much ambiguity, that it would be useful to state precisely the distinction between supernatural and miraculous, the very crux of the problem.

We would like to state here two clues to solving the problem:

1. Supernatural is not perceivable by itself, but by signs, clear yet obscure—(as in art).

2. Supernatural has to be situated in reference to the fundamental rapport of the first cause and the second cause, which are exercised at two levels (with some appropriate finalities and modalities): natural order and supernatural order.

1. SIGNS OF THE SUPERNATURAL

Signs and Proofs

Supernatural is not ordinarily miraculous, as we have said. It is but very exceptional, accessible not in itself but by signs, which visibly humbly manifest the invisible. It is because God is invisible and His essential action is equally invisible. The All-Powerful is discreet, and His essential action is equally discreet.

He does not proceed from the exterior, as is the human technique, but by the interior, as Creator. His signs are interior to life. They do not make any noise. They do not furnish material proofs, unless in limited cases, and even in those extreme cases these signs do not constrain human freedom and do not upset the ordinary procedures of science.

They are indications and a sensitive manifestation, not an intrusion nor a geometrical proof.

Supernatural is essentially the act by which God saves man and exalts him invisibly.

Mother Teresa is visibly penetrated by divine life; her life is love. She is radiant, effective, but there is nothing superman or superwoman about her. She remains as the ordinary little old woman who does not make any extraordinary miracles, but mobilizes hearts and bodies in the service of the poor. If one day we open her case for beatification we will probably have difficulty finding extraordinary miracles in her life; and nevertheless, it is clear that she is not inferior in holiness to her patron saint, Saint Theresa of Avila.

The most essential of the Supernatural is manifested by little signs devoid of the obvious and inexplicable characteristic, from which the word "miracle" gets its name.

Some Signs Most Often Ordinary

Supernatural is essentially given to mankind not by some exterior miracle, but by ordinary signs: baptismal water, bread and wine, gestures and words of a priest. We do not go as far as saying that Sacraments are not supernatural.

Holiness is an invisible act. It is accomplished essentially in the heart. It is invisible like God. It is the spiritual penetration of Divine Love which gives light and new meaning to life. It is discernible. Mother Teresa has been discerned on the international level of world leaders as being holy. What God does in her is discernible and even evident, but none of the human sciences has attempted to verify it because she does not lend herself to any material verification.

Charisms, which allow divine love to flow through human action are marked by the same discreet characteristic. God does not create them to burst forth with blinding lights like that of the singers of Hard Rock. Charisms awaken and elevate nature to the best of its capacities in the service of God and of mankind. But the action remains an ordinary human action, free, self-determined. Science will never be able to prove that a supplement of divine energy was inexplicably involved even though something of this nature occurred. The more man is clever in fabricating something spectacular, the more God flees from him. Even Jesus Himself would hide His miracles and would recommend discretion to the miraculously healed. The Church does the same, sometimes not without excess of prudence and mistrust.

Semi-Darkness (Le Clair obscur)

Well then, strictly speaking what about miracles? Will we object to: healings, signs in the sun, inexplicable fragrances that pilgrims experience in certain places of apparitions?

We touch here the case-limit where the supernatural manifests itself in an extraordinary way. But it is generally impossible to prove that it is inexplicable. Such a conclusion would contradict nature itself even in science, because the postulate of its research is that there is nothing inexplicable; that we must never resign in the face of the unexplained, but try to find an explanation until it makes sense. Fragrances, at any rate, escape any established fact. We could somehow consider them like a subjective phenomenon, an olfactory hallucination.

Similarly, the dancing sun. There, where the phenomena is filmed, this material document raises a question, but the scientific will think: This wierd image is due no doubt to the sun having disturbed a photoelectrical cell. If what the people have seen with their eyes, and what the film has been able to capture coincide (which is not easy to establish), will not a scientist provide an explicative hypothesis? In the face of science, miracles sometimes become probable, very probable, but there is always a loophole.

The same for healings. Hundreds of thousands of people have been healed in Lourdes and have given thanksgiving. For more than a century, thousands have testified to it, yet the proof that their healing was extraordinary was not established but 58 times in Lourdes. I say 58 and not 65, because the first seven healings in Lourdes have not been declared miracles in the mandate that recognizes the authenticity of apparitions. For these 58 recognized healings, there always have been doctors (even Catholic) included who have voted against—that proof did not appear irrefutable or absolute. Most of them refuse to declare the healing as inexplicable.

In short, here on earth supernatural remains "Le Clair obscur." God's signs remain invisible for the essential, like God Himself. They yield to the spectacular, to the inexplicable, to the miraculous, but only rarely, discreetly, in a disconcerting way which does not force human freedom to accept.

Miracle Over Magic

Permit me to insist: miracle is not magic, nor scientific performance. It is not advertised, nor is it obvious. God does not work on a spectacular and demonstrable register.

Moreover, He voluntarily lets us produce the striking "miracles" of our scientific "progress": speed, aerial and interplanetary navigation, instantaneous telecommunication, etc. They seemed like a dream two centuries ago, but now have been exalted as such. The miracles of God have another characteristic. They remain obscure. It is not surprising that most of the investigating commissions cannot find miracles in search of proof. It is the ordinary case in God's works, even authentic. The Pharisees did not obtain the proof that they demanded from Christ (*Matt.* 16:1; *Mark* 8:11; *Luke* 11:16).

An Interior Discernment

Then must we say: "An indiscernible miracle?"

Is it discernible, through convergent signs? This method of signs and convergences is not at all foreign to the sciences, whether they be historical, biological or even physical. Ordinarily, it starts with visible signs of a reality not perceivable, then science elaborates and verifies its hypothesis.

The discernment of the supernatural resembles, in many instances, that artistic discernment by which the validity of some music is qualified, and to promote the artistry of great musicians: Mozart, Bach, etc. It is the fruit of a discernment. In order to be able to discern music, we need to have a certain musical sense.

As to what concerns natural order, Paul the Apostle said it very well: "I wish their hearts to be strengthened and themselves to be closely united in love, enriched with full assurance by their knowledge of the mystery of God—namely Christ—in Whom every treasure of wisdom and knowledge is hidden" (*Col.* 2:3). Like musical sense allows music to penetrate, similarly the sense and the experience of God permits one to perceive His actions through discreet signs.

The supernatural is not a God-made machine, but a marvelous and gratifying blossoming of aptitudes and human forces, elevated to the best of their possibilities. God made us in His image. He wants to deify us secretly, in depth. And He gives us certain interior ways and means to discern it.

2. FIRST CAUSE AND SECOND CAUSES
A Mysterious and Diversified Relation

All these paradoxes hold forth to the very essence of the supernatural and to the very essence of divine action. And, it is difficult to understand not only because God is transcendent, but because His action is situated on two levels.

Transcendence of the First Cause

God, Who exists solely by Himself, is the first and exclusive Cause of all that exists at each moment. Nothing can exist without Him (*John* 1:2). We often misunderstand the mysterious relationship between the First Cause (God), and the second causes (His creatures). The first Cause (God) is invisible. Moreover, it is transcendent. It exceeds our means of knowing. Our surrounding is that of creatures, created things, thus of contingency.

The second causes (the creatures) are the only ones accessible to our perception, and to our scientific proofs. We can attain the first Cause only by philosophical ways. Scientific methods accede to the Big Bang theory and it is a prodigious conquest of knowledge. But what was there before the Big Bang? Why not something instead of nothing? Science does not have any answer to this profoundly human and philosophical question.

Relation Between the First Cause
and the Second Causes

The second causes are then of a different nature than the first Cause and are situated at a different level, and with heavy consequences.

We cannot add the first and second causes together. They penetrate each other. The first one penetrates and provokes the second. It gives it its very existence, including its autonomy and freedom, which are gifts from our Creator.

In fact, the classical theologians explained this original relationship by saying: God and man do not conjugate their strength like two created causes.

When two horses pull a cart, each does half the work, furnishes half the energy. When God cooperates with man, He does all the work and man does all the work, each on its own level. God is the Creator of all things that exist—all existence, but He gives exclusively to his free creatures' autonomy and a capacity to act which make them authentic agents and cooperators in His creation.

Natural and Supernatural Relation to God

This cooperation (this symbiosis) of the Creator and His creatures is therefore the most profound of the universe. It is infinitely diversified and not any less astonishing than the quantity is the quality and variety.

1. There is the rooting of each creature in the Creator Who gives him his existence. It is the level of nature.
2. There is the heightening (or raising) and divinization of the free creatures whom God calls to share His eternal life: It is the level of supernature...(supernatural).

This double presence of God is the object of two analogous and different experiences:

- Analogous, because it is the same God Who works in the natural order and in the supernatural order, in the same vital, interior, transcendent and sovereign way.
- Different, because at the supernatural level, God establishes a more intimate level, more personal and reciprocal —a friendly rapport (relationship).

God elevates and transfigures our nature; He allows it to participate in His very life, in His action of love and knowledge. It is a process for eternal life. It starts in this life, in laborious stages. God has healed us of sin and He has established in us a sharing of His love which is His very life. Love creates equal footing between those who love each other. This is why God's love gives a new dimension to our existence, at the level of His love.

It is this equality that Jesus Christ expressed in His speech at the Last Supper: *"I shall no longer call you servants,"* (what we are by nature) *"because a servant does not know what his master is about; I call you friends"* (*John* 15:15).

But He goes still further. He makes Himself our servant on earth. He has washed the feet of His disciples and in a parable on Heaven, He presented it thusly: He talked about the servants getting ready to welcome their master upon his return from a voyage. But what does the master do? He does not sit down at the master's place. Instead, he takes the apron of his subordinates to serve his good servants at the very same table they had prepared for him (*Luke* 12:37).

It is important to take note of this double fundamental relationship to God on these two levels.

First, on the level of **nature**, one must realize that the Creator gives us our very existence. On this level He is more intimate with us than we are with ourselves. This experience is not overwhelming but liberating if we are able to understand God at all, because God does not dominate our life, He creates it.

At the **supernatural** level, the summit, the experience of Christian mystics, this is where Bergson saw the best proof of the existence of God: a witness, evidence that it is not only verbal but in the transformation of their entire being. It is more frequent than we think in this central aspect of holiness. It implies the ontological experience of the Creator, but it accedes to a personal union with God, beyond sin, in a binding communion. God has saved us from sin and death by the grace of baptism and spiritual combat. He gives us His life which grows here on earth to become an eternal plenitude of love.

This experience cannot be egoistical and solitary. It radiates God's love for all His creatures, and an invitation to work for universal salvation by action (work) and prayer.

It is at this second level that the interior life (love) and the operational charisms flourish simultaneously to accomplish

God's work in the Church, and in this world. The paradoxical point of this cooperation is the miracle, often given exceptionally, to manifest God to so many who are blind and to so many others who turn a deaf ear, but never constraining them. Still, the miracle will never be but a diversified fact, an illustration of the history of Salvation by love.

God being the Creator of all, in over-abundance, we cannot do anything good without Him, freely, humbly, lovingly.

Where Man Becomes First Cause

Significant Corollary: Man cannot be first cause of being; God is the Universal Cause. But he can become first cause in wrong-doing (evil) because evil is nothingness, disconcentration of being, or deviation. All these detachments (defilements) do not reveal God. They are not God's work. Man's freedom gives him the formidable privilege of having the power of being first cause to amputate, paralyze, diminish God's work, through sin.

In this instance, man can be first cause: negative, deviant, destructive. He is pseudo creator in the order of nothingness.

Briefly, man is called to create with God. The most supreme creative act is when man and woman create, with God (the only Creator of the immortal soul), a new human being: a creative role that God did not grant to angels. Still, it is not the exclusive work of man; it is his most marvelous cooperation with God, as second cause.

On the contrary, man becomes first cause when he refuses or destroys this life which God gives him to create with Him.

Man can exalt himself in these destructive initiatives and the rage to destroy. It is in this vein that the perverse action of Satan, and that of his satellites, is situated.

3. APPLICATION OF THE SIGNS TO SCOTTSDALE

The grace of Scottsdale is situated in the supernatural order: spiritual combat and growth of the divine life, purification, participation in the creative work of regenerating grace and victory over sin. The humble voice of prayer in Scottsdale, where perpetual adoration developed spontaneously, and initiatives in service to others, visions, and charisms developed organically, are delightful signs. They remind us of important realities that our noisy world forgets. God is there. Jesus and Mary are there. They love us. They act; they help us. They need our answer to their love to overtake sin and save mankind. Scottsdale's grace is a sign. It is a mobilization, and a model for the edification of love.

This divine action satisfies ignorance, inspires initiatives, rectifies ideologies, and reconciles the faith of intellectuals. This coherent action of the Holy Spirit proceeded, not like an exterior mold, but like a light, an example, a living model. It edifies the Church and contributes in reconstructing the world not only by different and personalized graces, but also through the communities.

Among the authentic signs of this supernatural experience we cannot underline too much: humility, obedience (often difficult), sacrifice and union to the Passion of Our Lord, at St. Maria Goretti.

The experience of God, the awareness of His presence as Creator, constitutes the most profound of all psychoanalysis, if it is lived seriously, because it re-establishes contact with what is the most profound in us: the Creator Who has created us by love, for love. There is situated the principle and the very source of all regeneration.

Those who live this experience know its profound effects: uprooting of sin, going beyond interior divisions, a better perspective with respect to the near future, a more profound understanding of God and of others, interior peace and unity, and a hundredfold return promised by Jesus to those even here on earth who have given up everything (*Mark* 10:28-31). The special group at St. Maria Goretti attest to this.

Scottsdale Chronology

January 28, 1945 . . . . Birth of Fr. Jack Spaulding
March 12, 1957 . . . . Birth of Gianna Talone
January 22, 1958 . . . . Birth of Susan Evans
September 2, 1962 . . . . Birth of Stefanie Staab
May 18, 1963 . . . . Birth of Annie Ross
December 28, 1963 . . . . Birth of Mary Cook
August 6, 1966 . . . . Birth of Steve Nelson
May 26, 1968 . . . . Birth of Jimmy Kupanoff
August 15, 1969 . . . . Birth of Wendy Nelson
April 17, 1971 . . . . Birth of James Pauley
June 5, 1971 . . . . Ordination of Fr. Jack Spaulding
November 15, 1982 . . . . . Appointment of Fr. Jack Spaulding
as pastor of Saint Maria Goretti
Parish, Scottsdale, Arizona

1987

June 25: First pilgrimage of Fr. J. Spaulding to Medjugorje to film a television program.

September 16: Susan Evans' first visit to Fr. J. Spaulding.

October 7-15: Second pilgramage to Medjugorje by Fr. J. Spaulding with a group of parishioners.

November: Start of the Teen Prayer Group, ages: 13-19.

December 3: Start of the Our Lady's Prayer Group (Thursdays). First locution to Gianna.

1988

March: Third pilgrimage of Fr. J. Spaulding to Medjugorje.

Early Summer: First meeting between Stefanie Staab and Fr. J. Spaulding.

June 4-10: Fourth pilgrimage with Gianna, Carol Ameche and a group of parishioners.

June 6: Gianna claims vision of the Infant Jesus, and first message from Our Lady.

June 8: Vicka confirms Gianna's mission.

End of June: Gianna confides to Fr. J. Spaulding for the first time. Gianna receives a vision of the six (6) visionaries: Susan, Mary, Wendy, Steve, Jimmy and herself. And, in the background the three others whom she distinguishes less well: Stefanie, James and Annie Ross.

Beginning of July: Stefanie meets Gianna, who informs her of the gifts of God upon Scottsdale. A week later Steve confides his first locutions to Fr. J. Spaulding.

July 14: First reported public message of Our Lady to Gianna (Vol. I, page 109 of message books).

August 10: Gianna reports her first message from Jesus.

August 20: The Blessed Mother invites Susan and Stefanie to form a prayer group for young adults on Friday nights.

August: Fifth pilgrimage in honor of the closing of the Marian Year.

End of August: First meeting of the six (6): traded their experiences.

September 20: Gianna claims the first lessons from Jesus for publication (Vol. 1, page 9). First meeting of the total group of nine.

October: Our Lady informs Gianna that she will appear to her as well as to others.

October 28: Our Lord gives Gianna the message that will serve as the title of the book *"I Am Your Jesus of Mercy."*

End of November: First locutions received by Fr. Jack (not published). A week before, Gianna had told Fr. Jack that Our Lady would be speaking to him through the homily.

December 6: Start of Young Adults' Prayer Group.

December 28: Gianna claims apparition of Jesus.

1989

March 31: Locution of Our Lady to Annie Ross.

April 7: Second apparition of Jesus to Gianna, who has seen Him twice before seeing Our Lady.

May 23: Message received during Fr. Spaulding's homily published for the first time (Vol. I, pg. 131).

August: The start of the Commission Investigation.

October: Report of the Commission submitted to the Bishop.

December 19: First apparition of Our Lady in church at Thursday night prayer group as reported by Gianna.

December 20: Fr. Spaulding and Gianna see the Bishop.

December 28: First apparition of Our Lady to Annie Ross at the same time as Gianna.

1990

January 8: Declaration by the Bishop.

Easter: Gianna reports interior suffering—began during Lent.

April: Four visionaries now see Our Lady: Gianna, Wendy (once), Mary (two times), Annie, throughout 1990.

Autumn: At the Thursday night Prayer Group, the recitation of the Sorrowful Mysteries is replaced with the more brief and intense prayer of the Chaplet of Divine Mercy (from Sister Faustina).

1991

End of July: My first trip to Scottsdale.

August 31: Gianna and Annie participate in the Charismatic Convention in Anaheim.

September: Annie Ross is advised she will have apparitions only on her birthday and in time of need.

October: Gianna's trip to Rome and Assisi and a third apparition of Our Lord.

October 12: She meets the Pope and submits her message to him.

November 23: Annie calls off her approaching marriage (Dec. 21).

December 12: Our Lady reassures her on the compatibility of a human marriage.

1992

February 17: Marriage of Annie Ross.

May 4-8: My second trip to Scottsdale.

June: Publication of this book.